The Incredible
Sai Baba

Arthur Osborne was born in London and educated at Christ Church, Oxford. He was deeply interested in spirituality and spent several years at Ramanashram, the Ashram of the Sage Ramana Maharshi at Tiruvannamalai in South India. His other books are *Ramana Arunachala and Ramana Maharshi and The Path of Self-Knowledge*.

The Incredible
Sai Baba
The life and miracles of a modern-day saint

Arthur Osborne

Orient BlackSwan

All rights reserved. No part of this book may be modified, reproduced or utilised in any form, or by any means, electronic or mechanical, including photocopying, recording or by any information storage and retrieval system, in any form of binding or cover other than in which it is published, without permission in writing from the publisher.

The Incredible Sai Baba

ORIENT BLACKSWAN PRIVATE LIMITED

Registered Office
3-6-752 Himayatnagar, Hyderabad 500 029, Telangana, India
Email: centraloffice@orientblackswan.com

Other Offices
Bengaluru, Chennai, Guwahati, Hyderabad, Kolkata,
Mumbai, New Delhi, Noida, Patna,

© Orient Blackswan Private Limited

First published 1957
Reprinted 1970, 1973, 1974, 1975, 1980,
1985, 1988, 1990, 1992, 1993, 1994
Retypeset 2000
Reprinted, 2002, 2005, 2013, 2018, 2021, 2022, 2024

ISBN 978 81 250 0084 6

Printed in India at
B. B. Press
Tronica City Ghaziabad (UP) 201102

Published by
Orient Blackswan Private Limited
3-6-752 Himayatnagar, Hyderabad 500 029, Telangana, India
Email: info@orientblackswan.com

CONTENTS

	Foreword	vii
	Acknowledgements	ix
I	Introducing Sai Baba	1
II	The Guru and His Family	23
III	Hinduism and Islam	48
IV	Symbols and Powers	57
V	The Symbolism of Money	68
VI	Upadesa	78
VII	Death and Survival	90
	Continued Presence	97

FOREWORD

It is perfectly true, as the author remarks, that Sri Sai Baba, although well-known all over India, is not known outside India; especially in the Western countries. The author wishes to introduce him to the Western world. With this laudable object in view he has written this book which contains Sri Sai Baba's brief life, teachings, miracles and anecdotes. Although Sri Sai Baba's life, as depicted in the book based on authentic reports of his devotees, is strange and eccentric, no one who has come in contact with him and his devotees can deny the fact that he was, and Ramdas can say, he is, a saint of the highest spiritual eminence.

Ramdas had the privilege of visiting Shirdi about four years ago for the darshan of Baba's samadhi. He found that the atmosphere in the Mandir where the samadhi is located was vibrating with spiritual peace and joy. Sai Baba seems to be still living in that holy place. Another wonderful sight that met Ramdas's eyes was that a regular stream of devotees was pouring into the temple for the darshan of Baba's samadhi throughout the day. In Ramdas's wanderings in different parts of India and during his visit to the houses of devotees he also discovered everywhere pictures of Sai Baba adorning the walls. His popularity is so vast and wide that his name has become almost a household word among the people of India who hold him in the highest veneration. Sai Baba is a most potent spititual force that moulds and transforms the life of spiritual aspirants who seek his guidance and blessings even to this day.

The author, Sri Arthur Osborne, has done an invaluable service to the seekers of Truth in the West by presenting this book to the world. He has, in a spirit of love and devotion to Sai Baba, related the most important events in his life which stand out in bold perspective, conveying to the heart of the reader the pre-eminent glory of Sai Baba. Sai Baba's divine personality seems to have captured the heart of the author and he writes about him with such a spontaneity, giving details of the life and miracles culled from various sources, that he cannot but create in the heart of the reader a wave of admiration and devotion for this great spiritual master.

Ramdas earnestly wishes that this book should be in the hands of every spiritual aspirant and, for that matter, everyone, whether he is a believer or non-believer, so that he can know how God reveals Himself in the form of a unique and fully inspired saint of Sai Baba's stature. Sai Baba's sayings are quite original in their import and expression. The last quotation from Baba's sayings, as mentioned in this book, has charmed Ramdas and he will end this short foreword by giving it here: 'I give people what they want in the hope that they will begin to want what I want to give them.'

(Sd) Ramdas

Anandashram, Kanhangad
25th April, 1957

ACKNOWLEDGEMENT

Shortly after the death of Sai Baba the late Swami B. V. Narasimhaswami made a collection of his sayings and of anecdotes about him which he entitled *Shri Sai Baba's Charters and Sayings*. He also collected statements of their experience from a considerable number of devotees and published them in three volumes under the title *Devotees' Experiences of Sai Baba*. Both these books were published without copyright by the All India Sai Samaj at Madras, of which Swami Narasimhaswami was the President. I spoke to the Swami before his demise of my intention of writing a life of Sai Baba and he requested me to make full use of all the publications of the Samaj. I wish to acknowledge my indebtedness for the help I derived from these sources.

CHAPTER ONE

INTRODUCING SAI BABA

'Look, here comes the crazy fakir again!'

The shopkeepers turned and looked up the street at the tall, gaunt youth who was striding towards them, energetic but aloof, speaking to nobody.

No one knew who he was. He had first appeared in the little town of Shirdi as a lad of about sixteen in 1872, as wandering fakirs do, none knowing whence or why. He wandered away again, roamed about for a while, and then came back and spent the rest of his life there. During his earlier visits he lived under a neemtree, sitting there in the daytime, sleeping on the bare ground at night, eating what little food charitable townsfolk gave him. When he stopped wandering and settled down at Shirdi, he first went to a little Hindu temple there, intending to make it his abode, but the custodian, Mahalsapathy, who later became one of his closest disciples, regarded him as a Muslim fakir and refused him admission, bidding him go to the mosque to live. He did so, and the little mud-walled mosque remained his home.

He spoke with the holy men, Hindu or Muslim, who occasionally passed through the town, and one of them had told the townsfolk 'Watch that young fakir; he's a jewel on a dunghill.'

But they had not taken much notice. It seemed more likely to them that he was a bit cracked. He did not mix with them — scarcely spoke. He sometimes said *namaz* (the ritualistic Islamic prayer that has to be said five times a day) but very seldom. He had queer habits of his own too — he kept a fire burning perpetually in the little mosque — more like a Parsi than a Muslim — and he burned little oil lamps there.

Except for a handful of food, oil for the lamps was the only thing he needed and he used to go to the shopkeepers to beg for it. That was what he must be coming for now. One of them nudged the other: 'Let's have some fun with him; let's refuse to give him any oil.' A sprinkling of sightseers gathered round. Refused oil, the young fakir turned and went back with no word of complaint or beseeching.

'Let's follow him back and see what he'll do,' someone suggested. The old herd instinct of baiting the outsider was at work.

They soon saw. Arrived back at the mosque, the fakir picked up a mud pot of water that stood there and filled the lamps from it and they burned as with oil.

There was no nudging or tittering now. In sudden awe they fell at his feet and begged him not to curse them for what they had done.

No more talk of crazy fakirs. The people of Shirdi believed now in the jewel on the dunghill. They knew that they had a man of power among them. They soon found that he was a saint and teacher with enormous compassion for those who suffered.

Nevertheless, he remained bizarre, a man of mystery. Nobody knew his name. Sai Baba is not a name. Sai

Introducing Sai Baba

(pronounced approximately like 'sigh') is a Persian word for 'saint' and Baba is a Hindi term of endearment and respect meaning 'father'. Nobody knew why he chose Shirdi as his abode. Rather a village than a town, six miles from the nearest railway station, not previously a spiritual centre; and yet he remained there for nearly half a century, until his death in 1918, while ever more devotees flocked around from the towns. If there was a personal reason it was as strange as the whole circumstances of his life: many years later, when he was already famous, he told a devotee to dig at the foot of the neem tree where he used to sit on his first arrival there; a tomb was unearthed and he declared that it was that of his Guru, not in this life but in a previous incarnation.

So far as this life goes, practically nothing is known of his early years. It is fairly certain that he was born of a middle class Brahmin family in a small town in Hyderabad State. Possibly his parents died when he was young, because at a very early age he left home to follow a Muslim fakir. A few years later the fakir died and he joined a Hindu Guru. He was deeply attached to this Guru, whom he referred to by the affectionate diminutive of 'Venkusa'. He has told the story of how they met and of their life together.

'Once I was discussing the Puranas and other works we were reading with three friends and arguing how to attain realization.

'One said that we should depend on ourselves and not on a Guru, because the Gita says "Raise yourself".

'The second said that the main thing is to control the mind and keep it free from thoughts and doubts.

'The third said that forms are always changing and only the Formless is unchanging, so we must constantly make distinction between the Eternal and the transitory.

'The fourth disliked theory. He said: "Let us simply do our duty and surrender our whole life and body and speech to a Guru who is all-pervading. Faith in him is all that is needed."

'As we roamed through the forest we met a labourer who asked us where we were going in the heat of the day and warned us that we would get lost in the trackless thickets, and for no purpose. He invited us to stay and share his food, but we rejected his offer and advice and walked on. And in fact we did lose our way in that vast, dense forest.

'He met us a second time and said that we had got lost through trusting to our own skill and that we needed a guide. Again he invited us to share his food, telling us that such an offer was auspicious and should not be spurned; however we again declined his invitation and continued on our way. Only I felt hungry and went back and accepted a piece of bread from him and drank some water.

'Then the Guru appeared and asked what we were arguing about and I told him all about it. The others left him, showing him no respect, but I bowed down to him reverently. Then he took me to a well, tied my legs with a rope, and suspended me head downwards from a tree that was growing beside it. My head was about three feet above the water, so that I could not reach it. My Guru left me there and went away, I knew not where. He returned four or five hours later and asked me how I was getting on. I replied that I had passed my time in great bliss. He was delighted with me and embraced me, passing his hand over my head and body. He spoke to me with great love and made me his disciple, whereupon I entirely forgot my mother and father and all my desires.

'I loved to gaze on him. I had no eyes except for him. I did not want to go back. I forgot everything but the Guru. My whole life was concentrated in my sight and my sight on him. He was the object of my meditation. In silence I bowed down.'

This is a typical Sai Baba account because the whole story is symbolical. The forest is the jungle of the mind in which the quest for Truth takes place, and the four friends are four modes of approach. The labourer is the Guru and the food he offers is his Grace. 'The Guru appeared' means that after the youth has accepted the food he discovers that the giver of it really is the divine Guru. Therefore he bows reverently, that is accepts his authority. Tying him head downwards over a well is overturning the ego, binding it and holding it within sight of the cool waters of Peace. (Incidentally, this mode of discipline has been used physically by some Masters.) It is because of this that the ordeal is blissful; it is suffering beatified by the end for which it is endured. This absorption in the Guru is the *Sadhana* or Path followed and the final 'In silence I bowed down' is the extinction of the ego in Realization.

A Guru normally guides his disciples along the path that he himself has trodden, and therefore this account has importance with reference to Chapter Six, where Sai Baba's spiritual training of his devotes is considered.

On another occasion he said: 'After my fakir's death his widow left me with Venkusa at Selu. I stayed with with him for twelve years and then left Selu.' Even here the twelve may be merely symbolical of a completed period (the twelve signs of the zodiac). It can scarcely be literally true if Sai Baba was only sixteen when he first went to Shirdi after the death of his Guru. He is said to have been eight when he left home, and a few years with the fakir must be allowed.

It is characteristically bizarre that all his life he kept with him a common brick that his Guru had given him. When finally it dropped and broke in 1918, shortly before his death, he said: 'It is not the brick that is broken but my karma; I shall not survive its breaking.'

It is obviously not necessary to know about his early life or training. If it had been he would have told us.

It was about 1900, that Sai Baba's fame began to spread and since then it has continued. In a town as far distant as Madras you can walk down a bazaar street and in shop after shop see his bust or portrait, often with incense sticks burning before it. There is probably no Saint in India who has more devotees or whose cult is so widespread (a statement which does not include Rama or Krishna who are, strictly speaking, not Saints but Avatars).

Introducing Sai Baba

And yet Sai Baba is almost unknown outside India. To the best of my knowledge, no life of him has been published by any Western publisher in any European language.

Why such a discrepancy? I suggest that it is because Sai Baba does not accord with the modern conception of a Saint, that is, that he should lead a decorous life, not performing too many or too startling miracles, and should expound his teaching in philosophy on which the scholars can write theses, arguing that: 'for x the world was purely illusory, while for y it possessed an indisputable though transitory reality,' or some such rubbish; whereas in fact the great Sages speak from Knowledge not opinions, and any contradictions there may be between them are due either to the impossibility of expressing the Ineffable in words or to the choice of one viewpoint or another to suit a particular type of disciple. There are many different viewpoints of a mountain peak from its base and a Master may turn his light on one or another and on the path leading up from it; such paths, illumined by various Masters, may cross as they wind up the mountain side, so that the short-sighted geographer can prove that they run in opposite directions, but the Master knows the summit, which is one, and knows that they all lead there.

Sai Baba never wrote a book. His behaviour was bizarre. And he flaunted his miracles with the reckless exuberance of a child. No easy saint to introduce to the modern reader.

Not only did he not write books; he did not read them either. He did occasionally instruct a devotee to read some religious or scriptural work, but for the most part he discouraged them from reading, 'People hope to find Brahma in these books, but it is bhrama (confusion) not Brahma (God) that they find there.'

There is something unorthodox in such a statement. Some basic theoretical understanding is necessary except in very rare cases, but continued accumulation of theoretical knowledge does not help towards spiritual understanding. Indeed, mental study can distract a man from the more arduous task of spiritual effort with the false allure of an easy alternative. Particularly in this age, when such a flood of books are churned out, it is a danger. Shri Ramakrishna also neither practised nor enjoined scholarship. Bhagavan Ramana Maharshi, though enormously erudite, wrote in a derogatory way on book learning. 'It is the unlearned who are saved rather than those whose ego has not subsided despite their learning. The unlearned are saved from the unrelenting grip of self-infatuation, from the malady of a myraid whirling throughts, from the endless pursuit of (mental) wealth; it is not from one ill alone that they are saved.' ('Forty Verses', Supplement, v. 36.)

The unlearned state described here means, of course, not mere ignorance but the simplicity and integrity of mind which Taoism extols, which Christ designated as 'like a little child' which Islam implies in the illiteracy of the Prophet. It is not incompatible with learning; nevertheless learning cannot produce it and absorption in learning can destroy it.

For years it was doubted whether Sai Baba was ever literate; certainly nobody supposed that he knew Sanskrit.

Introducing Sai Baba

Then one day he gave an exposition which showed learning as well as the perspicacity and rough humour natural to him.

A devotee was massaging his legs and feet, chanting to himself meanwhile in an undertone. Sai Baba asked him what he was muttering.

'A Sanskrit verse,' he replied, not suspecting that Sai Baba knew enough scripture to want a more precise answer. However, he was asked what verse.

'A verse from the Gita.'

'Say it aloud.'

The devotee then recited in Sanskrit verse 34 of chapter IV: 'know that by means of prostration, enquiry and service the *Jnanis* (Enlightened) who have realized the Truth will teach you *Jnana* (Knowledge).'

'Do you understand this, Nana?' Baba asked him.

'Yes.'

'Then tell me the meaning.'

Nana gave a free rendering in the vernacular but Sai Baba was not satisfied. 'I don't want a paraphrase; I want the strict grammatical meaning, with case, mood and tense.'

Nana gave a literal translation, wondering the while whether Baba knew anything of Sanskrit grammar. He soon found out.

'In *tatviddhi*, what does *tat* stand for?' Baba asked him.

'*Jnana* (Knowledge).'

'What knowledge? Knowledge of what?'

The knowledge referred to in the previous stanzas.'

'What does *pranipat* mean?'

'Prostration.'

'And *pat?*'

'The same.'

'If they meant the same would Vyasa* have added two unnecessary syllables?'

'I don't see any difference between them,' Nana admitted.

Baba left that for a while and passed on to the next point.

'What does *prasna* mean?'

'Asking questions.'

'And *pariprasna*?'

'The same.'

'Then if they both mean the same was Vyasa off his head to use the longer?'

'I don't see any difference.'

'Next point. What does *seva* mean ?'

'Service such as I am doing now in massaging your feet.'

'Nothing more?'

'I don't see what more it can mean.'

'We'll leave that too. Next point. Krishna tells Arjuna to get *Jnana* (Knowledge) from *Jnanis* (the Enlightened). Wasn't Krishna himself a *Jnani?*'

'Yes.'

'Then why does he send Arjuna to others instead of giving him *Jnana* himself?'

---

*The legendary author of the Mahabharata, the epic in which the Bhagavad Gita is an episode.

'I don't know.'

'Wasn't Arjuna a *jiva* (being) and therefore an emanation of *Chaitanya* (Universal Consciousness)?'

'Yes.'

'Then how can Knowledge be given to what is already an emanation of Consciousness of Knowledge?'

Sai Baba then interpreted the verse to mean that it is not *Jnana* (Knowledge) but *ajnana* (non-knowledge or ignorance) that the Guru gives.

Nana, now thoroughly bewildered over what had seemed to him a straightforward verse, asked Sai Baba to expound these points.

He explained. 'The verse tells us how a disciple is to approach his Guru in order to attain Realization. He must completely surrender body, mind, soul and possessions to the Guru.* That is the prostration referred to. The enquiry must be a constant quest for Truth, not questions asked out of mere curiosity or for a wrong motive, such as to trap the Guru. The motive must be pure desire for spiritual progress and Realization. Then the service is not mere physical service such as massaging. For it to be effective there must be no idea that you are free to give or withhold service; you must feel that your body no longer belongs to you since you have surrendered it to the Guru and it exists only to do him service.'

Then followed a catechism on the Guru giving ignorance,

---

* Sai Baba himself did not demand the surrender of the property of his disciples; it is a question of attitude of mind: there must be complete readiness to surrender all.

'Isn't Brahma pure Knowledge or being?'

'Yes.'

'And everything else non-being or ignorance (non-Knowledge)?'

'Yes.'

'Don't the scriptures declare that Brahma is beyond the range of speech or mind?'

'Yes.'

'Then the speech of the Guru says is not Brahma or Knowledge?'

'No'.

'Then you admit that what the Guru says is not Knowledge but ignorance?'

'It seems so.'

'Then the Guru's instruction is simply a piece of ignorance used to remove the disciple's ignorance, just as we use a thorn to remove another thorn from the foot, isn't it?'

'I suppose so.'

'The disciple is a *jiva* (being) whose essential nature is Knowledge, isn't he?'

'Yes.'

'Then there is obviously no need to give him Knowledge but simply to remove the veil of ignorance that hides the existent Knowledge. This, of course, is not to be done at one stroke, since the disciple is immersed in age-old ignorance and needs repeated instruction, perhaps through life after life. And what is the nature of this instruction through speech about what is beyond speech? Isn't it like removing a cover? Ignorance conceals the pre-existent Knowledge just as water plants cover over the surface of a pond. Clear away the plants and you have the water. You don't have to create it; it is there already. Or take another example – a cataract grows on the eye and prevents a man from seeing; remove the cataract and he sees. Ignorance is the cataract. The universe is the efflorescence of the indescribable Maya, which is ignorance; yet ignorance is needed to illuminate and dissolve this ignorance'.

'Divine Knowledge is to be realized, not taught. Prostration, enquiry and service are the methods by which to obtain the Grace of the Guru.

'It is an illusion to suppose that phenomena are real. That is the screen of ignorance which hides Knowledge. Tear it off and Brahma or Knowledge will shine forth'.

'Ignorance is the seed of *samsara* (birth and death). Put the medicine of the Guru's Grace on the eye and the screen of Maya lifts, leaving only *Jnana* (Knowledge). *Jnana* is not something to be attained, it is eternal and self-existent. On the other hand, ignorance has a cause and an end. The root of it is the idea that the devotee is a separate being from God. Remove this and what remains is *Jnana*'.

'Now the question why Krishna referred Arjuna to other Gurus instead of giving him *Jnana* himself. Did Krishna consider other *Jnanis* separate from himself or their teaching different from his? No. So their teaching is his and there is no difference.'

Sai Baba then told Nana to bring the Bhagavad Gita and read a chapter before him each day and he would expound it. He did so – but no record was kept. A book whose vigour and profundity one can imagine from the above fragment simply evaporated and was never written down. Even this, however, is enough to show that when Sai Baba did talk theory it was the purest Advaita, the doctrine of Nonduality, that is the very essence of spiritual teaching.

Now the question of miracles. In recent times most Spiritual Masters have largely abstained from miracles. The more materialistic an age is, the more it is impressed by signs and wonders which (as Christ warned his followers and is universally recognized in India) are by no means always spiritual in provenance. Therefore the use of them is usually deemed inadvisable. Or perhaps it is presumptuous to say what the Master deems inadvisable or why and is better simply to state the fact that they are sparingly used. The Divine Grace may manifest in various ways the ambience of a great Saint or Master, but that is different. It does not imply open or deliberate acts. Devotees of Bhagavan Ramana Maharshi*, the supreme Sage of modern times, remarked how prayers to him were answered, sicknesses cured, dangers averted, although he overtly performed no miracle. When asked for an explanation of this he said that, 'It is enough for the thoughts of a *Jnani* to be turned in any direction and the automatic divine activity begins.' All such activity was as discreet and inconspicuous as possible.

---

* See my *"Ramana Maharshi and the Path of Self-Knowledge"*, published by Messers Riders & Co.

Introducing Sai Baba

But not so with Sai Baba. His miracles were flamboyant. Nothing automatic there. Two stories will serve to illustrate the difference.

A lady died at Tiruvannamalai. The bereaved husband could not take the body for cremation as rain was pouring down the whole day from a leaden sky; and in the Indian climate it is both unwise and illegal to keep a body more than twenty-four hours before burial or cremation. He went and told the Maharshi. Looking up at the sky the Maharshi said, as any one else might: 'I think it will clear up.' The devotee went back to his house and immediately ordered the bullocks to be yoked to the cart to take the body into town for cremation, such was his faith in every word the Maharshi said. And in fact the rain held off long enough for his purpose.

And now the other story.

Shirdi was some six miles from Kopergaon, the nearest railway station, and the only conveyance was a horse carriage. Some visitors to Sai Baba urgently needed to catch the night train in order to return to Bombay, but a terrific thunderstorm was raging. Sai Baba looked up and shouted: 'Hey! Enough of that! Stop it now! My children have to go back.' And the storm stopped.

However, there was purpose in his miracles. How varied the purpose will appear later in this book. He said: 'I give my devotees what they want so that they will begin to want what I want to give them.'

Even apart from his miracles, there was something bizarre about Sai Baba. A strange figure, teaching Hindus and Muslims alike, keeping a sacred fire burning in a mosque, raging at his devotees, even beating them with sticks, answering unspoken thoughts, flinging stones and abuse at an unbelieving visitor to drive him away or performing a miracle to attract him, openly asking for money and then giving it away to others, he was a spiritual Gargantua, one before whom Gargantua is dwarfed to a schoolboy. He would fly into a towering rage for no reason that could be seen, pouring out abuse, but the storm would pass and he would suddenly speak graciously to someone who had just arrived or was taking leave. He would repeat Islamic sacred phrases, Arabic or Persian, seldom or never Hindu, but in an undertone, as though not wishing to be heard.

He had strange rites too. He would stand before his ritual fire and rub coins together. One of his closest devotees, Das Ganu, has described this. 'Sai Baba occasionally performed strange rites between one and two in the afternoon at the mosque, alone and with a cloth screen in front of him. He would take out a purse of some ten or fifteen old coins of various denominations from a quarter anna to one rupee and rub them constantly but gently between his finger tips. I don't know whether he said any mantra meanwhile. Their surfaces were worn smooth by this. He would sometimes say, as he rubbed them, this is Nana's, this is Bapu's this is Kaka's and so on. But if anyone approached he would gather them up and put them back in the purse and hide them.'

Obviously the coins symbolised devotees on whom he

Introducing Sai Baba

was working spiritually, transmitting Grace, uplifting and supporting them. Every master does so, but Sai Baba used symbols where with another there might be no outer sign.

A Muslim devotee who was a personal attendant on Sai Baba has described another strange rite. 'Baba used to sit behind a pillar in which a lamp was ensconced and kept burning permanently. He usually sat behind the pillar, not in front of it, so that from where he sat the lamp was not visible. I never saw him gazing at the lamp. I used to fill mud pots with water and place them near him. He would sit with two of them beside him and keep on pouring out water in various directions. I can't say why he did it or whether he uttered any mantra the while.'

Once again, it must have been a symbol of the outflowing of Grace.

There was no greater peculiarity than his way of sleeping. For a large part of his life he slept on a plank, five feet long by one foot three inches broad, suspended from the roof by flimsy strips of old cloth. It was some six feet above the ground and a number of lamps were placed loosely upon it. Levitation must have been necessary not only to get on to it but to stay on without breaking the supports; and there can have been no normal sleep. Once when Das Ganu and a few others went to look at the plank he seized it in a fit of anger and broke it to pieces.

An explanation of this strange mode of sleep can be found from a very fundamental comment made by Mrs. Manager, a Parsi lady. 'One noticeable difference between Sai Baba and other saints struck me. I have visited other notable saints also and have seen them in a state of trance or *samadhi* in which they were entirely oblivious of their body. Then I have seen them recovering of their surroundings, knowing what is in our hearts and replying to our questions. But with Sai Baba there was this peculiar difference: he did not need to go into *samadhi* in order to achieve anything or to attain any higher status or knowledge. He was every moment exercising a dual consciousness, one actively utilising the ego called Sri Sai Baba and dealing with other egos in temporal or spiritual affairs and the other transcending all ego and abiding in the state of Universal Soul. He was constantly exercising and manifesting the powers and features proper to both states of consciousness. Other saints would forget their body and surroundings and then return to them, but Sai Baba was constantly both in and outside the material world. Others seemed to take pains and make efforts to read the contents of people's minds and tell them their past history, but with Sai Baba no effort was needed. He was always in the all knowing state.'

A Realized Man can, as Mrs. Manager says and as the present writer beheld in the case of Bhagavan Ramana Maharshi, be in a state of permanent *samadhi* or Divine Knowledge, and in such a case not only is trancelike *samadhi* unnecessary but normal sleep is also unnecessary. It is not the oblivion commonly known as sleep that he experiences but the luminosity of *samadhi*. This would mean that Sai Baba was not asleep at night but in a state of levitation and *samadhi*, watching over his devotees and sending out his Grace upon them. Why he should display this in a manner that seems exhibitionist and yet get angry at its being seen is another matter.

The profundity of Sai Baba and his oddity, the symbolism of his speech and the wildness of his manner is shown in a brush with authority that he had. A thief was arrested with stolen jewellery and brought before the magistrate's court in the neighbouring town of Dhulia. It would have been a simple case, only he brought forward the embarrassing plea that Sai Baba had given him the jewels. Every one knew that wealth was heaped upon Sai Baba daily and disbursed or distributed by him the same day; however, in this case it was definitely known that the jewels were stolen property. The only thing to do was to issue a summons to Sai Baba to attend the magistrate's court.

'Baba, here's a summons for you,' the police constable faltered timidly.

'Take that rag of paper and chuck it in the fire, one of you!' Baba roared. And one of them did.

Naturally, such flouting of authority could not be overlooked and a warrant had to be issued for his arrest. The constable advanced nervously with it. 'They've sent a warrant this time, Baba. Will you please come to Dhulia with me?'

With a torrent of oaths, Baba ordered him to throw it into the latrine.

Some of the more influential devotees gathered together to talk over what could be done. They drew up a petition to the effect that one who was worshipped by a vast following ought not to be summoned to a law court and praying that a commissioner should be sent to Shirdi instead to take down his evidence. This was conceded and one Joshi, a first-class magistrate, was sent.

'What is your name?' he began.
'They call me Sai Baba.'
'Your father's name?'
'Also Sai Baba.'
'Your Guru's name?'
'Venkusa.'
'Creed or religion?'
'Kabir.'
'Caste or community?'
'Parvardigar.'
'Age?'
'Lakhs of years.'

The routine questions to open an enquiry; only the answers to them were far from routine. They were all cryptic or symbolical. Sai Baba was not a name but an epithet, as already explained. By giving it as his father's name also he implied that he was no longer conditioned by human parentage. Kabir was a great poet-saint of the late 15th and early 16th century who had both Hindu and Muslim followers; by giving his name Sai Baba intimated that he also stood above the religions, at their source, and guided his followers on both paths. 'Parvardigar' is a Divine Name; it is recognized that one who has attained self-realization is above the four castes, in the divine state; this was the implication. As for the reply about his age, it implies that he was beyond the limitations of time, established in the eternal now of spiritual awareness.

Introducing Sai Baba

Coming on the heels of this, the next routine question must have sounded peculiarly apt: 'Will you swear that what you are going to say is the truth'?

'The truth', he affirmed briefly.

'Do you know the accused?'

'Yes, I know him.' That at least sounded satisfactory, but only until Sai Baba added: 'I know every one.'

'He says that he is your devotee and has stayed with you. Is that so?'

'Yes. All are with me. All are mine'. An affirmation of the universality of the Divine Man, but not much use as legal evidence.

'Did you give him some jewels, as alleged by him?'

'Yes, I gave them to him'. But once again the clear statement was bedevilled by metaphysics: 'Who gives what? And to whom?'

'If you gave him the jewels how did you get possession of them?'

'Everything is mine.'

The magistrate now lost his patience. All this might be good metaphysics but it was bad evidence. 'Baba!' he expostulated, 'this is a serious charge of theft. The man says that you delivered the jewels to him.'

Baba also lost patience. 'What is all this about? What the devil have I to do with it?' And he strode away.

Subsequently the question of giving evidence was dropped because it was discovered that the accused had not been at Shirdi at the time of the theft.

It is interesting to note that Sai Baba was not asked to sign his statement. He never signed any paper. He had no name to sign.

It was about 1900 that Sai Baba's fame began to spread. In the last decade of his life Shirdi was constantly thronged with visitors. The sick were healed, the childless obtained families, the doubting acquired faith. Towards the end magnificent annual celebrations were held with steed and chariot and caparisoned elephant, as for royalty. Sai Baba disliked all this pomp but gave into the importunity of his followers. Daily wealth poured in and was disbursed like water, so that when he came to die he had with him just as much money as was needed to cover his funeral expenses. Since his death the number of his devotees has increased, not diminished. How is it, then, that he has remained unknown in the wider world outside India?

I have indicated the answer already. There is a great deal of faith still remaining in India. There are holy men, though for the most part discreetly unknown. There are genuine sadhus and fakirs, wayfarers on the Path, as well as frauds. But there is another side of the picture also. Westernised, educated, urbanised India is captivated by Western ideals of science and progress, whether through democracy or Communism, and is very sensitive about being thought backward or superstitious. It is the products of this India who write books for foreign publishers and overseas sale. No wonder, then, that they shrink from proclaiming a saint who taught in miracles instead of books. Sai Baba's devotees are mostly found among the conservative types of people, (though one is apt to find the most surprising people privately numbered among them). Books enough have been written about him in the various Indian languages, but it is perhaps natural that it should have been left for a Westerner to make Sai Baba known to the West.

CHAPTER TWO

THE GURU AND HIS FAMILY

Bizarre, yes, but that should not blind us to his loving care for his devotees and the spiritual development he brought about in them, nor to the love and devotion they felt for him. It will perhaps be best, therefore, to open this chapter with a statement of this by one of his devotees, the Mrs. Manager already referred to.

'One's first impression of Sai Baba was of his eyes. There was such power and penetration in his gaze that no one could long look him in the eyes. One felt that he was reading one through and through. Soon one lowered one's eyes and bowed down. One felt that he was not only in one's heart but in every atom of one's body. A few words or a gesture would reveal to one that Sai Baba knew all about the past and present and even the future and about everything else. There was nothing else to do but to submit trustfully and surrender oneself to him. And he was there to look after every minute detail and guide one through every vicissitude of life.'

It is his love and protection, the spiritual exaltation of his presence, that she emphasises. 'It was not merely his power that endeared him to his devotees. His loving care combined with his powers to make Shirdi a veritable paradise to those devotees who went there. Directly we arrived there we felt safe, that nothing could harm us. When I went and sat in his presence I always forgot my pain, and indeed the body itself and all mundane cares and anxieties. Hours would pass while I sat blissfully unaware of their passage. It was an extraordinary experience shared, I believe, by all his real devotees. He was all in all and the All for us.'

Another devotee, Y. J. Galwankar, speaks especially of the purifying nature of Sai Baba's influence. 'I first visited Sai Baba in 1911. I went because my father-in-law and other relatives were going. I had heard of Sai Baba's saintliness but was not at that time seriously drawn to seek either spiritual or temporal benefits from him. I visited him in this way four or five times and my interest gradually increased. Then he appeared to me in a dream and asked me for two rupees *dakshina* (alms). On waking I decided to pay this and sent two rupees to him at Shirdi by money order. In the same dream he gave me two valuable instructions, first to behave with probity and integrity and secondly to maintain chastity. I have observed these instructions with care and zeal. Once, after this, when I went to Shirdi, about 1917, he put his hand over my head and this had a strange effect on me. I forgot myself and my surroundings and fell into a state of ecstasy. I learned afterwards that while I was in that state Sai Baba was telling those present that I was characterised by integrity and purity. He described to them various forms and conditions that I had passed through in previous lives and said that he had placed me in my mother's womb in this birth and I had still retained my integrity and purity.'

The demand for two rupees was a form of symbolism much used by Sai Baba. He was demanding the two coins of purity and integrity.

The Guru and his Family

Sometimes he appeared to people in dreams or visions to draw them to him. Always it is the Master who draws his followers, although it may appear to be their decision or to be mere chance that one is chosen and another not. Sai Baba was explicit about this. 'I draw my people to me from long distances in many ways. It is I who seek them out and bring them to me; they do not come of their own accord. Even though they may be thousands of miles away, I draw them to me, like a bird with a string tied to its foot.' Many, of course, went merely because of the stream of miracles, in hope of worldly benefits. Some such, however, gradually developed a craving for the higher wealth that Sai Baba distributed. 'My people first come to me for temporal benefits, but when these are obtained they begin to follow me.'

One devotee, seeing the motley crowd assembled there, asked Sai Baba whether all of them derived benefit, a question that might be asked of any Master whose destiny it is to be publicly known. For reply he pointed to a mangotree in blossom: 'What a splendid crop it would be if all the blossoms turned into fruit, but do they? Most of them fall off. Very few remain.'

R. B. Purandhare was one of the blossoms that ripened into fruit. He has left an account of his first coming. 'I first heard of Sai Baba in 1909 and went to see him. I went with no worldly motives, though I was poor and an orphan. I was always desirous of associating with sadhus and felt drawn to him because I had heard that he was a saint. He appeared to me in a dream and summoned me to Shirdi. At the time my daughter (aged about six months) was very ill, so my mother objected to my going. Nevertheless, I persisted and took my mother and wife and the child with me. I stayed there for thirteen days and on the third day the child recovered from her sickness. Baba did not allow me to go back until the thirteenth day. I did not ask him about anything, but he told my mother that he had been connected with me for seven centuries and would never forget me however far away I was and would not eat a morsel of food without me.

'With Baba's permission, I left for Nasik and from there returned to our home at Dadar. On arrival there my wife got an attack of cholera and the doctor gave her up as hopeless. Then I saw Sai Baba standing beside the little temple opposite my house and he told me to give her the *udhi* (sacred ashes) that I had brought back from Shirdi. I did so and within half an hour she recovered sufficient warmth for the doctor to be hopeful. Soon she was all right.'

Some, of course, arrived without faith, just to see what the strange wonder-worker looked like. One such was an Anglo-Indian station master from a nearby town. On arrival he found Sai Baba washing out mud pots and placing them mouth downwards on the ground. He asked him why he was doing that and Baba replied with caustic humour, referring to unreceptive listeners: 'Pots come to me like that, mouth downwards.'

Deshpande, a devotee to whom there will be frequent reference, tells of an uncle of his who did not at first believe. Several times he went to see for himself, but Sai Baba threw stones at him and would not even let him come near the mosque.

The Guru and his Family

On other occasions Sai Baba suddenly broke down a visitor's prejudices in some equally startling way. A Brahmin doctor was once taken to Shirdi but warned his companion in advance that he would not bow down to Sai Baba, since he worshipped Sri Rama and no other. He stood outside the mosque, watching the Hindu ritual that was being performed inside, and then suddenly he rushed in and fell at Sai Baba's feet. When asked later what had made him change his mind he said that he saw Sai Baba standing there in the form of Rama.

This was not a case of rejection like the previous two but only of ignorant confinement of belief to one manifestation of God and therefore merited guidance; guidance was given, but the method of it was typical of Sai Baba. Another Master might have explained that all Gurus are One in so far as all manifest the One Self and draw devotees back to the One, but in all things Sai Baba was picturesque; he taught in symbols, not words. Therefore, instead of saying this he demonstrated it, revealing himself in the form the visitor worshipped.

This was by no means the only occasion when he gave such a demonstration. For instance, there was a similar case with a caste-proud Brahmin from Nasik. Before this man's arrival at Shirdi, Baba suddenly called out for some ochre dye to colour his robe. However, he did not in fact dye it or wear ochre; he always wore white and continued to do so now. The Brahmin arrived and stood at some distance from the mosque for fear of pollution. Suddenly he rushed into the mosque and fell at Sai Baba's feet. He had seen there not Sai Baba but his own ochre-robed Guru.

Once a devotee was won over, Sai Baba did not let go of him. He said: 'When one of mine dies, even though it be a thousand miles away, I draw him to myself just as we draw a sparrow with a thread tied to its foot. I will not allow my man to get away from me.' From me? From Grace. It was giving, not taking, drawing back from distraction to Unity, from the world to the Spirit.

He showed a detailed knowledge of the thoughts and actions of his devotees, past and present, at Shirdi and far away, that must have been disconcerting at times. And the word 'showed' is not used conventionally here; he displayed it, flaunted it.

A typical case, with its cogent humour, concerned over-rigid orthodoxy. Sai Baba did not approve of extremes of orthodoxy, such as refusal to eat onions. A devotee, by name S. B. Nachne, tells the story. 'I went to Shirdi in 1915 with a party that included my mother-in-law. We put up at Sathe Wada (as it was then called; it has since changed hands and become Navalkar Wada). Dada Kelkar was occupying a part of the premises. My mother-in-law began cutting up onions to cook with our food, but Dada was a strictly orthodox Brahmin who could not stand onions. He lost his temper and railed at my mother-in-law, and she took this very much to heart.

'A few hours later Dada's granddaughter developed a severe pain in her eyes and began to cry. Dada went straight to Sai Baba and asked him to cure it. Sai Baba, who had been told nothing about the quarrel, told him to rub the child's eyes with onion. He asked where he was to get it from. Sai Baba always had some with him and perhaps Dada hoped for some that he had touched, but instead he pointed to my mother-in-law and said "Get it from her".

What is noteworthy is that it never for a moment entered the minds of the devotees to doubt that such a bizarre cure would work if prescribed by Sai Baba.

On the arrival of a devotee, Sai Baba might regale the company with a story of what had happened to him, sometimes telling the story in the first person, identifying himself with the devotee, sometimes impersonally, not mentioning to whom it had happened. It might be a long and circumstantial story or just a brief allusion.

Of the latter type there was an example with Adam Dalali, a Muslim follower. Sometime previously a poor Marwari had come to his house to ask for food and he had given him four annas (quite enough for a meal in those days) and sent him to a Marwari hotel. When he went to Shirdi Sai Baba immediately said: 'I went to this man's house and he sent me to a Marwari hotel.'

It was in the healing of sickness that Sai Baba's powers were the most lavishly displayed. At first he used to prescribe various herbs; then one day he told the attendant who dispensed them not to bother about herbs any more but to give everyone the same medicine. For a while he gave sublimate of alum to all comers and they were cured. After some time, however, the *udhi* or sacred ash from Sai Baba's fire began to be used. Sai Baba himself often worked cures without any physical support, but at a distance his devotees used the *udhi* with effect and still do.

To record all Sai Baba's miraculous cures would be an impossible task. Almost every devotee has recollection of them, and even apart from those that took place before witnesses at Shirdi there are those that were and still are effected at a distance through prayer to him. Here only a few typical ones are described. It will be seen that in some of them there is a fantastic display of power over and beyond the simple cure.

Joseph, a Roman Catholic police officer, has recorded: I never went to Shirdi but I have heard of Sai Baba from friends and I have his picture with me. I don't worship the picture but I regard him as a saint. He had great power.

Joseph adds in his explanation that his patron saint is St. Francis Xavier but that he prays to Sai Baba also and his prayers are answered.

'In 1917 Norvekar fell ill. His son took Rs. 500 and paid it to Baba. On receiving it Baba began to shiver with fever. When asked why, he said, "When we do anything for others we have to take the burden and responsibility on ourselves." Soon after this Norvekar recovered from his fever.'

Sai Baba's acceptance of money in such a case is another peculiar feature. Normally a man who performs spiritual cures refuses all reward. In some cases the power leaves him if he takes rewards. Actually, there was no question of 'reward' in Sai Baba's case, since he never kept the money; nevertheless his treatment of money was unusual and will be dealt with in a separate chapter.

Deshpande, whose uncle had lacked faith, had a blind grandfather. In 1916 he took him to Shirdi and led him by the hand to Sai Baba.

The old man bowed down before him and simply said: 'Baba, I can't see.'

'You will,' Baba replied. 'Give me four rupees.'

Again the demand for money, though ridiculously small sum. Deshpande went out to change a note and when he returned with the four rupees, Sai Baba simply laid his hand on the old man's head and his sight was restored. When he cried out in wonder and praise, Baba simply bade him to take *udhi* and go. In leaving a holy man or a shrine the taking of *udhi* is customary.

Another case, perhaps more surprising, is recorded when a blind woman cried out: 'Baba I want to see you with these eyes!' Immediately she was able to see, but no sooner did she go out from his presence than her blindness returned. What she asked for had been granted.

In 1913 B. U. Bahalkar's little son had high fever for five or six days and the doctor told him there was little hope. Bahalkar then down and prayed to Sai Baba (the Hindu normally prays sitting crosslegged, not kneeling). At two o'clock in the night Sai Baba appeared in his room, applied *udhi* to the child and said: 'There's no more need to worry. In two hours the boy will perspire and in the morning he will feel better. When he is quite well bring him to me.' Of course, it happened as he said.

This was on 3 March in Bahalkar's house at Dhulia. Two days later he received a letter from Deshpande, who was staying at Shirdi, in which he wrote that Sai Baba had said to him: 'I have been to your Dhulia friend's house.' Deshpande had asked him what friend and he replied, 'Upasani Bahalkar.

I go to his house daily. You had better write to him.'

Once, in the typically flamboyant style, Sai Baba said to Mahalsapathy, a resident devotee: 'Your wife has a very painful tumour on her neck. I will cure it. No one else will cure it, only I.'

Mahalsapathy's wife was not at Shirdi at the time and he did not even know that she had a tumour. Later he received a letter about it and its sudden cure.

The following might be called a test case.

M. W. Pradhan, a Justice of Peace, has related how his young son, Babu, fell ill. They had in their house a Telugu priest who, as is not uncommon in well-to-do families, performed all the ritual worship for them. This priest, Madhava Bhat, was strongly attached to the family but was not a devotee of Sai Baba. On the contrary, he thought the child's sickness might be a punishment for worshipping one whom he considered a Muslim. He, therefore, asked the parents to go and make a vow to Datta (an Aspect of God which they worshipped) and pray for the child's recovery, but they told him that Sai Baba was Datta. One night he saw in a dream a figure that he recognized from the picture in the house as Sai Baba, sitting at the top of the staircase, with a short stick in his hand. In the dream Sai Baba said to him: 'What do you mean? I am the Lord of this house.'

Bhat kept the dream to himself, but the child's condition continued to get worse. Finally he could stand the strain no longer and running to the picture of Sai Baba, he cried out: 'If the child improves enough to be brought downstairs by four o'clock this afternoon I will agree that you are Datta.'

The Guru and his Family

The temperature began to go down and by four o'clock the boy himself asked his mother to take him downstairs and let him play.

And finally a case where the sickness was not merely cured but foreseen.

S. S. D. Nimonkar, a police inspector, was on his way from Poona to Nimon where his brother's wife had recently given birth to a child. He stopped at Shirdi on the way to see Sai Baba. As he was taking leave, Sai Baba gave him the usual *udhi*, saying to him: 'Save the child's life.'

On his arrival at Nimon he found the newborn child all but dead. Breathing had almost stopped and the parents had lost hope. He looked for the *udhi* that he had given but could not find it. He must have lost it on the way. Nevertheless, he took the child on his lap and prayed to Sai Baba for help, and within fifteen minutes the crisis had passed and the child began to recover.

Sai Baba's help was also manifested frequently in giving issue to the childless. As with most things, the method was symbolical. Usually he would give a coconut in token of fertility; sometimes some other fruit. On one occasion it was the breaking of a coconut that and he showed reluctance; several times putting it aside until at last a devotee persuaded him.

D. S. Rasane, having no children, married a second wife, but this marriage also remained barren. It should be explained in parenthesis that, even before the new law forbidding polygamy, the enormous majority of Hindus were monogamous, but if a man had no son to perform the funeral rites for him he could take a second wife with the consent of the first.

One day, on Rasane's arrival at Shirdi, Sai Baba immediately handed him four mangoes and, addressing him by the diminutive of his first name, said: 'Damia, take these mangoes, eat them and die.'

Symbolical as usual. Rasane was taken aback until it was explained to him by others there that to beget a son is equivalent to dying and being replaced by another. To plunge into the life of the world is death; to remain calm and aloof is life.

Baba continued: 'Don't eat them yourself; give them to your wife.'

'Which wife?' he asked.

'The second. Let her eat them and she will have two sons. The first is to be named Daulat Shah and the second Thana Shah.'

Later Sai Baba told him that he would have eight children in all, which proved true. On the birth of his first son he came to Sai Baba and asked what name to give it. Despite all the people he had met and all that had happened in between, Sai Baba instantly replied: 'Have you forgotten what I told you? You wrote it on page three of your notebook. Didn't I tell you he was to be called Daulat Shah?'

There was a complicated case with one Sapatnekar extending over many years. A spiritual Master has enormous patience. It is no use trying to pick unripe fruit, and he will wait patiently through the years for it to ripen. Sai Baba was first brought to Sapatnekar's notice when he was a young man taking his law examinations. He turned to a friend who was notoriously

The Guru and his Family 35

weak in studies and, rather unkindly, asked him how he expected to fare. The friend replied with complete confidence that he would pass because he had Sai Baba's assurance. Sapatnekar made fun both of his friend and Sai Baba and predicted the worst. Actually, the friend did pass but Sapatnekar was not convinced; he regarded it as a lucky chance. He himself passed, set up as a lawyer, married and had a son.

Ten years later his son died and he had no other child. He remembered the way he had spoken about Sai Baba and began to worry about it, wondering whether his son's death was in retribution. He decided to go and see him and apologize. Sai Baba, however, shouted roughly at him and drove him away at sight. Again he came and bowed down and again he was driven away.

About a year later, however, Sai Baba appeared to his wife in a dream and invited them both to go to him. This time Sapatnekar was received graciously and apologized for his past contempt. Sai Baba then turned to someone who was standing by and told the story of Sapatnekar's life in the first person, as though it was his own. Then pointing at him, he said: 'This man blames me because he thinks I killed his son, but now I am going to bring that same soul back into his wife's womb.'

When he was taking leave, Sai Baba gave him a coconut and bade him to tie it in his wife's shawl and go away rejoicing. A year later he brought to Sai Baba the child that had been born.

Another devotee, L. G. Munge, had several children but they all died in infancy. He went to Sai Baba and complained of his misfortune, praying for one son that would live. Baba immediately replied: 'Why do you ask me for one? I'll give you two.'

And in fact he got two sons and two daughters.

But a condition for granting these favours was faith and submission. We have seen in the case of Sapatnekar how Sai Baba waited until the submission had matured. And now an instance where it was lacking.

It was some time in 1910. Suddenly one morning Sai Baba burst out; 'What is the scoundrel coming to see me for? What have I got? I'm just a naked fakir with human organs, like anyone else.'

It was one of those outbursts when no one knew what he was referring to. A little later, however, a couple of official carriages drew up with their escort outside the mosque. The wife of the District Revenue Commissioner, an English lady, had long hoped for a child and now thought she would try the wonder-working fakir whom all the Indians were talking about. She was accompanied by her husband and by the Collector (a title which, in British India, signified the local administrative officer, the most important man in the district).

They looked round uneasily. This base, primitive environment was no setting for members of the ruling class. The Assistant Commissioner, who had accompanied them, saw a devotee waiting about in the yard outside the mosque and, calling to him, bade him ask Sai Baba to finish his morning routine quickly as the sahibs wished to speak to him.

The devotee was aghast. Binding as the word of a sahib was, he could not take such a message to Sai Baba. He did

The Guru and his Family

not even pretend to do so but declared outright that it was impossible. If they had any business with Sai Baba they must await his pleasure.

It was half an hour before he was free and came that way. The lady stepped up to him and, bowing, said politely, 'We wish to have a little talk with you, Maharaj.'

However, such politeness was not enough for Sai Baba. It was not the heartfelt devotion he required. He said roughly: 'You must wait half an hour; I have to go and beg.'

All his life, however, much wealth flowed in, Sai Baba retained his custom of begging his food. Actually, he went only to a few houses which considered it an honour to feed him, and sometimes he delegated a devotee to beg for him. To make the white sahibs wait while a fakir begged his food was a lesson in humility typical of his bizarre humour. Also, it was open to them to remove the necessity for begging by contributing or obtaining supplies for him if they had thought of doing so.

It was not half an hour but only ten minutes later when he returned. Again the lady bowed and repeated her request.

'Wait an hour longer,' he replied.

The officers of government had not the time. Nor were they disposed to be made fools of in this way by a mere fakir. They got into their carriages and rode away, and the lady remained childless.

Cures for the sick and children for the barren were the most frequent benefits, but whether it was an examination to pass, a job to obtain, a lawsuit to win or a marriage to arrange, devotees, would appeal to Sai Baba, and if the request for aid was made with faith and sincerity it was likely to be granted.

'So much can easily be said of Sai Baba by all, by mere observers from the outside,' explained G. G. Narke, a professor of geology at the Deccan Gymkhana College of Engineering and a devotee to whom we shall often have to refer for a deeper interpretation of Sai Baba. 'But any one who judged him from the outside like this was very far out in his appraisal. Baba was, of course, adapting himself to the capacity for understanding of the people who came to him for help and protection. Most of them were superficial and sought only material benefits, and to them he did not reveal his inner nature. But when one capable of diving deeper came to him he revealed more of himself and his true powers.'

Sometimes, in performing a miracle, he would say 'I will do this.' More often, however, his reply would be *'Allah achcha karega'* (God will put it right) or *'Allah Malik hai'* (God is the Ruler). It was a peculiar custom of his to refer to God as 'the Fakir', and when refusing a request he would often say: 'The Fakir will not let me do that' or 'I can only do what the Fakir orders me to.'

He often did refuse. Sometimes he would explain that to prolong the life of a sick person would only cause prolonged suffering. Sometimes he would promise to bring him back in a new birth. Sometimes when asked to bless with issue he would say that there was no child in that person's destiny (not that this always deterred him, for at least on one occasion he granted a child out of his own destiny, declaring that there

The Guru and his Family

was none in that of the petitioner). Sometimes he would give no explanation at all but simply refuse, saying '*Allah Malik hai*' or 'The Fakir will not let me.'

B. A. Patel was a landowner and revenue officer. His aged father had a stroke. He went to Sai Baba to ask for *udhi* for him, but Sai Baba said: 'I will not give you *udhi*, *Allah Malik hai*.'

Three days later the father died.

This Patel was very proud of his physical strength. It was in 1913, when Sai Baba was already old and frail, and Patel would often massage his legs and then pick him up bodily and carry him to the fire. One day, soon after his father's death, he tried to do this but was utterly unable to move him. Baba laughed at him and Patel records: 'He taught me two things, not to be proud of my strength and not to grieve for my father.'

Sai Baba said to him: 'Why should you grieve? In five months he will return.' In five months a son was born to Patel. There is the plain meaning that this was the rebirth of his father or the profounder meaning that the life force which had taken on a form to which he was attached would do so again, since he had failed to destroy attachment at its roots.

A woman's young son was bitten by a cobra and she cried out and begged Sai Baba for *udhi* but he did not give it and the child died.

H. S. Dixit, one of the oldest of the devotees, implored him: 'Baba, her crying to hear-rending. For my sake revive her son.'

Here again, as in the incident of curing a child's eyes with onion, it is striking to see that there was never the slightest doubt that he could do this.

Sai Baba replied: 'Do not get entangled in this. What has happened is for the best. He has entered another body in which he can do specially good work which he could not do in this one. If I draw him back into this body then the new one he has entered will have to die for this to live. I might do it for your sake, but have you considered the consequences? Have you any idea of the responsibility and are you prepared to assume it?'

Death to one form is always birth to another except in the case of the *Jnani*, the fully Enlightened or Self-realized Sage who passes beyond forms to the Formless Infinite which is spoken of as Moksha or Nirvana.

S. B. Mohile had a daughter with a hare-lip and took her to Sai Baba, hoping he would cure her. As soon as he arrived Sai Baba said: 'I know what your have come for but it would be useless. The girl is of divine nature (daivi) and her life on earth will be short. Next Nagha Shudda Chathuri Day she will die. If you go to your office on that day and do not stay at home you will not see her again.'

It happened so. She died on that day while her father, who had ignored the warning, was at his office.

At least one case is recorded when Sai Baba wrestled in vain for a life. There was an outbreak of bubonic plague in Nigoj village and the wife of the Patil or squire had fallen ill. Sai Baba was passing that night at the *chavadi* or resthouse with Mahalsapathy in attendance.

'Don't sleep tonight,' Sai Baba bade him. 'Stand and keep watch for me the whole night because I have to pray to God. That ruffian (the plague) wants to kill the woman, so I am praying to Allah.'

Mahalsapathy kept watch through the night to prevent any disturbance but just before morning an official arrived with a body of servants. They made a great commotion, shouting that he wanted *darshan* (an interview) with Sai Baba. Mahalsapathy tried to quieten them by giving them *udhi* but in vain. Sai Baba burst forth from the rest-house in a raging temper. Shouting and abusing Mahalsapathy, he cried: 'Are you the father of a family? Don't you know what is happening in Nigoj? Why do you admit people at such a time?' Then suddenly he was calm. 'So be it. What has happened is right.'

And that morning the Patil's wife died.

Despite the many favours he granted, Sai Baba could be a hard master. There were few who escaped his blows or abuse. And it was not necessary for a selfish thought to crystallise in speech or action for it to be punished. The thought itself was enough.

A devotee has told how he was sitting there when someone brought a present of pink bananas, a variety with a rare flavour that grows only at a certain altitude in the hills. Seeing Sai Baba peeling them and giving them away, he felt an involuntary fear that they would all be finished before his turn came. Sai Baba immediately peeled another, gave it to someone else, and threw him the skin, bidding him eat that. He did so, accepting it meekly as a punishment for his greed. Sai Baba was pleased at this and, peeling another banana, shared it with him.

A muslim woman who kept purdah bowed down at Sai Baba's feet, unveiling her face. A devotee sitting beside him observed how beautiful she was and felt a hope that she would show her face again. Without a word, Sai Baba swung round and dealt him a blow with his stick.

A leper clambered slowly up the steps to the mosque. He was filthy and almost naked, covered with sores and stinking of rotting flesh. His feet were affected by the disease, so it seemed to take ages for him to approach Sai Baba and prostrate himself before him. Then he turned to go and when at last he was down the steps the elegant Mrs. Manager felt a wave of relief. Sai Baba sent a devotee to call him back. Again the slow clambering up the steps, the tottering nearer, the foul stench. This time, as he prostrated himself, Sai Baba picked up a dirty cloth bundle that he had been carrying and opened it. Milk sweets! Good! He took one and, of all those present, gave one to Mrs. Manager. Such was her devotion that she ate it without demur.

One test of faith was when devotees were not allowed to leave Shirdi on the date they had planned. It was the practice, as with any other Guru, to ask permission to leave, but he did not always grant it. If the devotee's leave of absence was due to expire or if he had some business or other appointment, this could be very awkward. None ever suffered by it. Somehow matters turned out so that no harm was done; but great faith was needed to believe that beforehand.

H. V. Sathe has related a typical instance. He was serving on a committee with the Revenue Commissioner of whom we have already heard, and the Collector. They were due to meet

The Guru and his Family

at Manmad and set out from there on a tour of inspection. On the day before they were to meet Sathe sent his father-in-law to Sai Baba to ask leave for him to depart. But Sai Baba refused. Sathe told his father-in-law that he could not trifle with important official engagements or he might be thrown out of government service altogether. Again the elder man went to ask permission and again Sai Baba refused, even ordering him to lock Sathe in his room if he tried to go.

It was three days before he was allowed to leave for Manmad. On arrival there he found that the other members of the committee had altered the original programme and postponed the meeting. On the strength of the original programme he had ordered his tent and equipment to be sent to Manmad but by a strange inadvertance this had not been done. 'So by my detention at Shirdi I lost absolutely nothing except my peace of mind and was saved a lot of unnecessary trouble and enabled to spend more time with my family and with Sai Baba. Of course, Sai Baba knew and arranged all this, but in my ignorance I was very uneasy about staying at Shirdi. Such instances strengthen one's faith in Sai Baba and reliance on him.'

It can further be added that if his faith had been stronger he would not have lost his peace of mind.

It was quite safe to stay at Shirdi when Sai Baba ordered it; it was by leaving without permission that a man invited trouble. The following case of Abdur Rahim Shamsuddin Rangari, a Muslim devotee, illustrates that.

'In 1913 there was plague at Thana, where I lived, and also, I think, at Shirdi. My wife had been suffering for a month from some disease. Her throat and cheek were swollen and she could eat nothing. She was taking medicine but it did not help her. A Hindu neighbour, R. G. Gupta, a lawyer, advised me to take her to Sai Baba at Shirdi, as that would cure her.

'When we started out, she was unable to swallow anything, but by the time we reached Igatpuri she could take tea and by Nasik she could eat something. This was a good omen. She was improving rapidly. On reaching Shirdi I went to the mosque and bowed down before Sai Baba. He asked me in Hindustani where I had come from and why and told me to bring my wife to the mosque.

'I took her up the steps and she bowed before him. He put his hand on her head and said '*Khuda achcha karega*' (God will put it right). I gave him one rupee four annas without being asked and he accepted it and gave me *udhi*. I stayed there for two hours. My wife's swelling was subsiding fast, so we started back at once without taking leave of Sai Baba. He had told me to stay, but since a cure had been effected I thought we might as well start. I did not like to stay in a strange place longer than necessary, especially with my wife and two-year-old son.

'The *tonga* (carriage) in which we had come was still in the village, so we took it and started back for Kopergaon, about six miles away. We had gone about half the distance when the axel of the *tonga* broke and we were left stranded on the road. It was about ten o'clock at night and there was no traffic. We could neither walk forward nor back such a distance at night. It was a lonely road and our predicament was unenviable, exposed to the night weather and in danger of highwaymen who infested the roads. We repented now our disregard of Sai Baba's words.

'Two hours passed in this way and then we heard the rattle of a carriage approaching and a voice calling out: "Where is the fellow from Thana?" A *tonga* came up to us and, seeing that it was the driver who was calling out I told him that I was from Thana and asked how he knew our plight and happened to arrive there at such an unusual hour. He said that Sai Baba had sent him.

"What for?" I asked him.

"To fetch you," he replied.

'So we got into the *tonga* and went back to Shirdi. It was between one and two o'clock in the morning when we arrived there. Baba was waiting for us at the mosque. He said: "You left without permission; that's why you had this trouble."

'I admitted it and asked his forgiveness. He made us stay near the mosque for the rest of the night while he went in and carried on his usual meditation. In the morning he went out to beg and came back with some bread and vegetables, of which he took a part and gave the rest to us. My wife was able to eat solid food. Then he gave us leave to go... This was my only visit to Shirdi but it gave me firm faith in Sai Baba.'

All these signs and wonders attracted people, but it was for spiritual benefit that the permanent devotees looked. Nor did they always have to go to Shirdi. He would say to them:'I am not confined to Shirdi or to this body, I am everywhere. I am with you whenever you think of me.'

Physically he never left Shirdi. One devotee tells how, when he was getting married, his father implored Sai Baba to attend the ceremony. He replied: 'Never fear; I am with you. Wherever you are I am with you if you think of me.' When further pressed he said: 'Without God's permission I can do nothing.'

Spiritual development was the real boon. Rao Sahib Y. J. Galwankar, who has been quoted already in this connection, says: 'When he placed his hand over my head it had an extraordinary effect on me. I forgot myself and my surroundings and passed into an ecstatic condition.... After this ecstasy I began to pay more attention to the spiritual side of life. Then came the second stage in 1932 (i.e. fourteen years after Sai Baba's death–author), when Baba appeared to me in a dream and asked me what I wanted. I replied that I wanted *Prem* (Divine Love) and that alone. Baba blessed me with *Prem* and disappeared. Ever since then I have had spells of *Prem* gushing through me when I am in meditation or even when I am reading or doing something else.'

To counter balance the impression left by outer wonders and an eccentric manner, let this, chapter end as it began with a devotee's impression of Sai Baba, this time Rao Bahadur S. B. Dhumal, a Brahmin and an advocate.

'I have one great difficulty when asked what are my experiences of Sai Baba. That is that at all hours of the day and night I am having experience of him. There is no incident in my life that I do not connect with him, however trivial it may appear to be. I firmly believe that everything in my life is swayed by Baba. What, then, is to be mentioned as my experience of him? Of course, the outside world will not be prepared to credit my belief, but that does not matter to me.

The Guru and his Family

In fact, the very disbelief of people seems a valid reason for refusing to disclose one's experiences. Every devotee feels that his experiences are his own and are given to him for his spiritual and temporal benefit and not for ventilation or publication to the general public.... The best way of understanding Baba is to experience him oneself. Where is Baba gone? He is still alive and active - more active, if it were possible, than he was before his *Mahasamadhi* (absorption in Nirvana). Anyone who is in real earnest can get in touch with him today and at once. But one who will not do that but seeks experiences at second or third hand will get very poor stuff.'

CHAPTER THREE

HINDUISM AND ISLAM

SAI BABA sometimes spoke of himself as a reincarnation of Kabir, the poet-saint of the late fifteenth and early sixteenth century who had both Hindu and Muslim disciples and taught each in the terms of their own religion. This is what he himself did. In his own behaviour he did not conform fully to either. He made his abode in the Shirdi mosque and generally used the Islamic name for God, and when he was heard to repeat mantras or sacred phrases they were Islamic, not Hindu; however, he very seldom said the ritualistic Islamic daily prayers. Some devotees never saw him do so; others report that he occasionally did on Saturdays or on some special occasion. Why Saturdays is one of the puzzles of Sai Baba, since it is Friday that is the day for corporate prayer among the Muslims. He was a vegetarian, like his Hindu followers and was worshipped by them in Hindu fashion; also he referred frequently to his Hindu Guru and to Hindu scriptures and Gods (that is forms and aspects of God).

He did not, however, encourage a merging of the two paths among his followers. He expected goodwill and tolerance between them; that was all. Although he did not say *namaz* (the daily prayers) he expected his Muslim followers to do so. Also both religions being valid, he did not approve of conversions from one to another but expected each person to strive in that in which he had been brought up. A Hindu who had been converted to Islam came to the mosque and Sai Baba slapped his face, exclaiming: 'So you have got yourself a new father!'

As a sign of goodwill, he liked his Hindu and Muslim followers to rejoice in one another's festivities (as has long been the custom in India) though, of course, without actually participating in the worship. So, for instance, a Hindu devotee tells how there would be a procession on the birth anniversary of Sri Rama, after which the Hindus would sing sacred songs interspersed by Muslim reading of the Quran. Sometimes also the Muslims would take out a procession bearing the shoes of Sai Baba on a cushion before them (so as to avoid anthoropomorphism or representational worship) and the Hindus would accompany them.

Apart even from any specific teaching, the mere influence of Sai Baba's presence led to goodwill and tolerance. The following story by a Pathan Muslim called Abdullah illustrates this.

'I left my home town of Tarbella when I was still a boy. I had no one to look after me. I wanted to go abroad and see Mecca and other places. I travelled south as far as Manmad where some one took an interest in me and told me that I could easily make my way to Bombay and from there get a passage to Mecca. Some one else, however, told me that there was a great man called Sai Baba at Shirdi who showered money on fakirs and would send me to Mecca if I wanted, so I went to Shirdi.

'As I entered the gate of the mosque Sai Baba was standing there before me. Our eyes met and I felt at once that he was my Guru. I stayed on at Shirdi. He fed me and other fakirs abundantly and I decided to stay there and lead an easy life. This was in 1913 when I was still quite young and had not begun to take life seriously. Nevertheless, my stay with Sai Baba brought about a marked change in my attitude of mind. When I first came to Shirdi I looked upon Hindus as my enemies but after I had been about three years with Sai Baba this feeling of animosity passed away and I began to regard them as brothers.'

Naturally, there was not always goodwill or understanding. It was the Hindus' worship of Sai Baba that was the stumbling block for Muslims, and the performance of this worship in a mosque seemed to be adding insult to injury.

Islam expresses the point of view that God alone is to be worshipped and that the whole universe was evoked by Him out of nothingness and all men are as nothing before Him. Hinduism expresses the point of view that the universe with all its beings is a form assumed by Him, a manifestation of Him, without, however, changing or detracting from His unmanifested Reality. To say that God created the universe out of nothing or that the universe is nothing but an illusion veiling the Reality of God comes to the same. The two points of view are therefore two aspects of the same truth, two ways of saying the same thing. Since a man has no reality other than that given by God, the essence of his being, the reality of him, must be that Reality other than which there is nothing, that is to say God. By realizing the nothingness of his individuality, by what was called in Medieval Christendom 'self-naughting' a man realizes the universality of his Divine

Hinduism and Islam

Essence. Therefore a man who has realized his true Self (which has nothing to do with psychology but goes beyond the mind to the very essence of Being and is without doubt the true meaning of the Delphic 'Know Thyself') has realized his essential Oneness with God ('I and my Father are One') beyond the accident of form. Appreciating this, Hindus worship such a one as God. Adhering to the letter of the law, most Muslims condemn such worship as idolatry. Actually it is not; it is not worshipping other than God but, on the contrary, recognizing that the worshipped has destroyed the illusion of otherness from God which still veils the worshipper.

All this is understood by the Sufis, who are the spiritual elect of Islam and of whom are the great Islamic saints. They teach in secret what the Hindus teach openly. But the esoteric Muslims do not understand. For them there is an absolute gulf between the two viewpoints, and for them the Hindus are pantheists or idolators. The Sufi poet, Al Hallaj used to proclaim when in a stage of ecstasy *'An' al Haq'*, 'I am the truth.' 'The Truth' is a Divine Name and he was executed for blasphemy in accordance with Islamic law, although the Sufis understood and have continued to revere him. Another Sufi, Abu Said, skirted the law, declaring negatively: 'There is nothing beneath this robe other than Allah.' A Sufi incantation used commonly to this day runs: 'I seek pardon of God for all (in me) that is not God.'

The Hindu worship of Sai Baba started very simply in 1908 with a child's homage to him. A Hindu lady tells the story. 'My brother Bapu Rao, who was then a child of four, used to go every morning and put a flower on Sai Baba's head and worship him. That was the beginning of the regular worship of Baba, as he had not permitted others to do it before that.'

The child was simply honouring Sai Baba as he had seen idols being honoured in temple worship; and from that time the practice spread of doing full ritualistic worship as to an idol. An intelligent Hindu does not believe that an idol is God any more than an intelligent Catholic believes that a holy picture or a statue of a saint is God. Few people are capable of conceiving of the Formless Absolute (are the critics of idolatry?), and the ordinary Hindu makes worship easier by concentrating on the manifestation of God in a certain form and aspect characterised by a certain picture or statue. He may be led thereby in due course to realization of the Formless, whether in this life or beyond it. It is said in the Gita: 'Whatever form a man worships, he really worships Me.' As ritualistic worship, with flowers and sandal paste is performed for an idol, so also it is for one who is felt to be more than a saint, one who has realized his identity with Supreme Being and is therefore a conscious manifestation of God.

Not all the Muslims at Shirdi could appreciate this, especially when the worship took place in a mosque. The result was that Muslim followers came to be far outnumbered by the Hindus. Occasionally also there were protests. One Rohilla Muslim who was constantly with Sai Baba and would sit and read the Quran at his feet at night protested against allowing the midday Hindu worship with its music in the mosque, Baba only smiled and said: 'All that is Allah.'

Hinduism and Islam 53

Puzzled over it as he would, it seemed to the poor man that Sai Baba was betraying Islam and he decided that he must make retribution. One day, when Sai Baba was out walking, he came up behind him with a club, intending to strike him down. Sai Baba turned just at that moment, touched his left wrist and looked at him. Under the force of this gaze he sank to the ground, powerless to lift the club or even to rise. Some one came and helped him up. A few days later he went and took leave of Sai Baba and, with his blessings, left Shirdi for good.

On another occasion a Muslim follower, Mir Jaman, sprang up suddenly at night and, drawing his sword declared that the Hindus were spoiling Sai Baba by worshipping him and asked permission to cut their throats. Sai Baba pacified him, saying: 'It is I who am mad and am responsible for their worshipping me, so if you want to cut any throats you must begin with mine.'

To the Hindus tolerance comes far easier. Their religion itself recognizes many forms of doctrine and ways of approach to God, not conflicting like Muslim or Christian sects, but recognizing each other as legitimate and suited to various temperaments and levels of understanding; they find it easier, therefore, to recognize the paths afforded in other religions. Hindu devotees worshipped the Divine Man in Sai Baba, and if Muslims did not, that was their concern. There were, of course, bigoted Hindus as well as Muslims, but their bigotry took a milder form. It injured only themselves, being expressed simply as refusal to worship a 'Muslim' Guru. Cases of such prejudice have been quoted already and of how they were overcome. The following story, like that of the Muslim Abdullah quoted above, illustrates the silent influence.

The deputy collector H. V. Sathe met a devout but simple-minded Brahmin called Megha, in whom he took an interest. He had him instructed in mantrams and sent him to Broach to worship Shiva there. After some time he told him that Sai Baba was Shiva incarnate and sent him to Shirdi to worship him. Megha, however, heard at the railway station that Baba was a Muslim and, horrified at the idea of prostrating himself before a Muslim, begged to be excused from going there. Sathe insisted, so he made the journey, albeit reluctantly.

Even before he reached the mosque, Sai Baba shouted angrily: 'Throw that scoundrel out!' and chased him away. He also turned angrily on Sathe and berated him for sending such a crude and narrow person.

That was outwardly, but inwardly the influence began working. A year or so later Megha felt genuinely drawn to Shirdi and this time he was not driven away but entered the mosque and stayed there. As with Abdullah, the inner change took place without verbal instruction. He served Sai Baba and conducted worship there daily, and when he died Sai Baba said: 'This was a true devotee of mine.'

More and more the Hindus predominated. Even the renovation of the mosque was carried out by them. When Sai Baba first took up his abode there it was a dilapidated mud structure with walls only eight feet high by fourteen feet long running round three sides, while the east side stood open to wind and rain. About half the roof had caved in and the rest was sagging and liable to fall.

Sai Baba could not be persuaded to live anywhere else, though his devotees would gladly have built a house or temple for him, so they decided to rebuild the mosque. Several times they asked permission but he refused. Finally one of them, G. R. Gundu, a Revenue Inspector who had obtained a son through Sai Baba's blessing, brought cartloads of stone and dumped them in front of the mosque, declaring that he was going to start work on it. Sai Baba told him to take the stones away and use them to renovate the local Hindu temples but he did not. Finally Baba allowed himself to be persuaded and the work began. Even then he interfered constantly and often pulled down what had been done. It was only at night that steady, uninterrupted work could be done, and not every night either. He used to sleep alternate nights in the mosque and the guest house, and his nights in the latter were the time for work. He insisted on proper Islamic architecture, with minarets and a nimbar or recess in the west wall (that is the wall facing Mecca) and steps supporting lamps. However, he also had a *dhuni* or fire-place where a perpetual fire was burning. Over against this he had a seat made for himself with a low balustrade to lean on. The mosque was thus a mixture of orthodoxy and innovation. He used to refer to it as a 'Brahmin mosque', though this did not necessarily mean 'Hindu' since he used the word 'Brahmin' in its correct sense of 'spiritual elect.'

In the centre of the yard outside the mosque he had a 'tulsi Brindhaban' constructed, that is a masonry block about three feet high containing a tulsi plant, sacred to the Hindus, for them to circumambulate according to tradition. Inside the mosque were grinding stones and Sai Baba used to spend much of his time grinding wheat into flour. This seemed to be one of his symbolical occupations, though he would bake a sort of cake with the flour in an oven outside the mosque and distribute it freely.

He also kept mud pots in the mosque or just outside it, from which he used to pour water, as described in a previous chapter, and others in which he used to put the food he begged. This was kept outside the mosque and the sweeper woman (the lowest of the castes) was allowed to take what she liked out of it before he ate, as also were dogs, crows or any who came.

CHAPTER FOUR

SYMBOLS AND POWERS

Symbolism is not an invention of any religion or Teacher but a recognition of correspondences that do in fact exist between the physical universe and spiritual Reality. The world actually is a reflection of higher reality, and therefore the symbols only have to be recognized, not invented. That is the meaning of the Hermetic dictum, 'as above, so below'. When Christ speaks of a man being born again or the Church speaks of the 'spouse of Christ' the symbolism is too evident to need explanation. It is said in the Quran: 'In the creation of the heavens and earth and the alternation of night and day and the ships that ply the sea with profit for men and the rain that God sends down from heaven, therewith reviving the earth after it is dead, and his scattering abroad in it all manner of beasts, and the turning about of the winds and clouds driven between heaven and earth - surely there are signs for a people who understand.' (ch. II v.164). To illustrate just one point from this passage: the falling of rain on barren land is a natural equivalent of the descent of Grace on a barren heart, awakening stirrings of spiritual life.

On the direct path of Advaita symbolism may be less in use, because the universe is rather negated than interpreted, but its existence is recognized, and on other paths it is extensively developed.

Nevertheless though all Teachers use symbolism, it can be said that Sai Baba was peculiarly addicted to it. There was something secret and mysterious about his teaching. Material benefits were conferred openly in the miracles he performed, but spiritual guidance was more concealed. Also, as has been remarked in earlier chapters, he frequently taught in actions where another might in words. For instance, whereas Christ said: 'Inasmuch as you do it to one of the least of these you do it also to me,' Sai Baba did not say it but illustrated it. A lady once asked him to come and take food with her and he consented. As may be imagined, she prepared special dishes with all the love and skill she had. She gave a gasp of horror when she saw a stray dog making for the food just before everything was ready. However, she drove it away in time and went to invite Sai Baba. 'No,' he said, 'you drove me away when I wanted it: now I don't want it.'

Even in trivial matters he spoke symbolically. A lady describes her first visit, when she was about eighteen. A devotee's spectacles fell off as he was bowing down and some one suggested that as they had fallen at Sai Baba's feet they should be presented to him. He immediately retorted: 'I don't need spectacles; I've got a pair. They cost forty rupees.'

Every one knew that he did not wear spectacles. The lady who told the story was puzzled until her father explained to her that by spectacles he meant sight or realization and by forty rupees the forty years since he had attained realization. He often spoke symbolically in performing cures, or as in the case when he gave a devotee four mangoes in token of children he would have and then added symbolism to symbolism by saying: 'Eat and die'. Once Deshpande, a devotee who has been mentioned already, was bitten by a snake and, in his terror, rushed straight to the mosque. When he reached the steps, however, Baba shouted: 'Don't come up Brahmin! Go back! Get down.' Even in his fear of death he did not dare disobey Sai Baba but stood there in mute supplication. A moment later Baba spoke again, this time in a gentle, kindly voice: 'Come up now. The Fakir is gracious to you. You will recover.'

'The Fakir', as already explained, was Sai Baba's way of referring to God. Deshpande now found that in the command not to come up Baba had been speaking not to him but to the poison which was entering his blood-stream.

He would sometimes speak in parables, leaving his devotees to work out the answer.

'Some robbers came and took away my money. I said nothing but quietly followed them and killed them and so recovered my money.' The money is the faculties natural to man in his pure state, to Primordial Man or Adam before the Fall; the robbers are the desires: killing them and recovering the wealth is destroying desires and realizing the Self.

'A man who had a very fine horse but, no matter what he did, it would not run in harness. An expert suggested that it should be taken back to the place whence it had come. This was done and it became tractable and useful.' The horse is the ego. As the commander of the physical and mental powers of man, it is useful, but it is self-willed and therefore makes endless trouble. Taking it back to its source is re-absorbing it in the Spirit or Self from which it arises. This is the same as Christ's saying that a man must return to his mother's womb and be born again; it is the same as Bhagavan Ramana Maharshi's cryptic injunction to one who asked the way: 'Go back the way you came.' It is the return to the

Source which purifies and enlightens. From there the ego issues forth again no longer an ego but a conscious agent of the Spirit.

He said to a woman follower: 'The sky is cloudy. It will rain. The crop will grow and ripen. Then the clouds will disperse. Why are you afraid?'

The overclouded sky is her present state of gloom and ignorance. The rain is the hardship and discomfort that she will undergo, but is also the Divine Grace that will ripen the seeds of spirituality in her heart, unknown to her, during the 'dark night of the soul'. The dispersal of the clouds is the attainment of light and bliss when the seed has ripened.

Sai Baba often gave cryptic replies which would seem meaningless to one who did not understand. Someone wanted to take a photograph of him and he replied: 'No, he is not to take a photograph. It is enough if he knocks the wall down.' Meaningless? A photograph is the likeness of Sai Baba. The wall is the I-am-the-body idea which stands between a man and his identity with the Spirit. It is enough to destroy that and the true likeness of Sai Baba will appear - not the body but the Spirit.

Another peculiarity of Sai Baba was that instead of answering a question directly he would sometimes refer the questioner to someone else or give him the answer indirectly. A case in point is quoted by Madhava Bua. He had thought, while sitting before Sai Baba, that the latter ought to explain to him the nature of one who is above the castes, that is the natural orders or categories of man. Baba suddenly turned to him and bade him go and read scripture with Dixit. He did so and found Dixit reading a passage which contained the very explanation he desired. A number of other devotes have told similar stories: how they were sent to one person or another and found him just reading or speaking about the question that was disturbing them.

In other ways also his instruction could be cryptic or hidden. Professor Narke says: 'He had the peculiar art of giving information to particular individuals in the midst of a group in a way that they alone could understand and not the other members of the group. Strangely enough, at one and the same time he could and did benefit many people by a few words or acts.'

None of this, of course, is exclusive to Sai Baba. In the ambience of a Spiritual Master the meaningfulness of the universe is automatically heightened, coincidences occur and signs appear. Nevertheless, all such things were apt to be more vivid and spectacular with Sai Baba than in other cases.

Prof. Narke has said: 'To one deeply observing him the startling fact came out into greater and greater prominence that Baba was living and operating in other worlds also besides this world and in an invisible body. Remarks made by him openly would be treated as meaningless ranting by those who did not know him. His language was also highly cryptic - full of symbology, parable, allegory and metaphor.'

Of the cryptic speech we have had examples enough. If someone asked permission to take a photograph and was told to knock a wall down he might well think it meaningless ranting. With regard to powers also, Professor Narke was by no means alone in believing that Sai Baba had power to guide the dead as well as the still embodied. There were those too who believed that he belonged to a hidden spiritual hierarchy and travelled at will in the subtle body. The village schoolmaster lived in the little mud-walled schoolroom just behind the mosque and he reports often hearing conversations there at night in strange languages, not only Indian languages but English also, of which Sai Baba knew nothing.

Physically he never left Shirdi, and yet when asked to go with devotees or to visit them he might answer : 'Yes I will go with you; I don't need a train to travel by.'

Again to quote the professor: – 'Baba frequently spoke of his travels with an invisible body over great distances of space (and time). Sitting near his fire in the morning with several devotees, he would say to what distant place he had been overnight and what he had done there. Those who had slept beside him all night at the mosque or rest-house knew that his physical body had remained at Shirdi the whole night. But his statements were literally true and were sometimes verified and proved true.... This power to travel in an invisible body to distant parts of this world, to traverse other realms than the earth-life and control what takes place there and to see the past and future alike revealed one great fact about his nature. Some of his own observations also demonstrated it. I have heard him say: "Where am I? Where is this world?" I have seen him point to his body and say: "This is my house. I am not here. My Guru has taken me away." As even in the flesh, in this earthly life, he was not confined to his physical body, it may truly be said of him that he is alive. He is where he was then; even then he was where he is now.... Sai Baba

Symbols and Powers

never spoke untruth, never spoke meaningless jargon, but only those who were familiar with his ways could make out the meaning of what he said or did - that is when it was intended for their understanding.'

And now two examples of Sai Baba's travels - that is of the sort of travels that could be checked.

A lady devotee has told the following story; and as she spoke she was so overcome with emotion that she could not restrain her tears. 'Baba's kindness to me was very great. My husband never went to see him, but even to him he showed great kindness. He was an engineer and about 1909 he was working on a bridge at Pandharpur. While he was living there I went to stay with Baba at Shirdi and served him. One day Baba told me I had better go to Pandharpur. He told me to start at once and added that he would go with me and there was no difficulty for him in travelling. So I started out. I did not know what had happened there. On arrival I found that my husband was not there. He had resigned his job and gone to Bombay. This was complete news to me and I was very upset. I had taken two companions with me and had only a few rupees. I had just enough to take us back as far as Kurdwadi, so we went there. I was really worried and was brooding over the situation. Suddenly a fakir appeared before me and asked me what I was worrying about, but I did not answer. He told me that my husband was at Dhond and that I should go there at once with my two companions. I asked him where the railway fare was to come from and he immediately handed me three tickets to Dhond and went away. Then, with my two companions, I boarded the train for Dhond.

'Meanwhile, my husband was having tea at Dhond and sitting in a half dreaming, half dozing state when a fakir appeared before him and said: "How is it that you are neglecting my mother? She is arriving on the next train in carriage No. so and so."

'He sprang to his feet, startled, and exclaimed: "Who are you to take me to task?" But the fakir had disappeared. When I alighted from the train my husband was waiting on the platform to meet me and take me to our new home. He told me about the fakir's appearance and asked to see a photograph of Sai Baba. On seeing it he recognized him as the fakir.

Now another such story, given this time by S. B. Nachne.

'In 1909 some events took place which at the time seemed to have nothing to do with Sai Baba. My elder brother was undergoing an operation at Bajekar's hospital in Bombay and we were all anxious about it. I was living at Dahanu then. That day a sadhu* came and asked me for a piece of bread. We invited him into the house and gave him a full meal. My sister-in-law served him all the dishes except ladies' fingers (an Indian vegetable) which she did not consider good enough to offer to a holy and honoured guest. However, the sadhu himself asked for ladies' fingers, so it was served. He blessed us all before leaving and told us that the operation had been successful.

'The same day my friend H. M. Panse told me that he hoped the operation would be successful by the grace of Sai Baba. That was the first time I ever heard of Sai Baba.

---

* 'Fakir' and 'Sadhu' both mean religious mendicant, only the former is a Muslim and the latter a Hindu.

Symbols and Powers

'Later in the evening my father returned from the hospital and we learnt from him that the operation had been successful and that there were no complications. After the operation a sadhu had appeared and, approaching the patient, passed his hands over the operated part and over the whole body and had said that everything would be all right.

'My brother recovered and had no setback.

'It was in 1912 that I first went to Shirdi.... During my stay there, Sai Baba showed great interest in me and my family. In the presence of Dixit, Jog and Dabolkar (three of the older devotees) he said, pointing to me: "I went to that man's house and he did not give me ladies' fingers."

'My mind immediately darted back to the sadhu who had dined with us at the time of my brother's operation and I felt sure that Baba was interested in our welfare and was helping us as early as 1909 without our knowledge. I told the devotees the incident of the ladies' fingers. That sadhu had quite a different appearance from Sai Baba. I saw him for about two or three days after the operation and had the opportunity of observing him at close quarters. After that he left Dahanu and was not seen there again.'

How are we to understand these incidents? Did Sai Baba actually materialise in the form of strange fakirs and sadhus or did he merely influence them from a distance to act in accordance with his will? It is noteworthy that to people who had seen him he usually appeared in a strange form whereas to those who had not he more often appeared in his own - as though considering the additional work of disguise unnecessary. Though there were instances (of which one has been related in this book) when he appeared in his own likeness to those who knew him also.

But if he assumed the forms of strange fakirs did he also assume the form of the dog that was driven away from the food? It is not necessary to postulate this. It is also possible that he simply knew what was happening and said in his picturesque way: 'Inasmuch as you do it even to a stray dog you do it also to me.'

There is another animal story, however, that is not so easily explained. A Brahmin devotee complained of dyspepsia and Sai Baba ordered him to stop taking sour curds, a favourite Indian dish. The devotee, however, was unable to give it up. The sour curds continued and the dyspepsia continued. One day a stray cat ate his curds. It returned next day and although it was chased away before it had eaten much, the Brahmin considered the rest polluted and had to throw it away. He took to hanging his curds in a bowl from a rafter across the roof. The cat took to climbing on to the rafter and still got at the curds. One evening the Brahmin lay in wait with a stick and as soon as he saw the cat on the rafter hurled it, striking the creature across the shoulder.

When he went to the mosque next morning Sai Baba was sitting among the devotees rubbing a weald on his shoulder and grumbling : 'They make themselves ill with eating curds, so you take it away, and then they beat you.'

Even so, it is possible to suggest that Sai Baba inspired the cat's actions and then healed its wound, taking the burden on himself. This often happens. An example has been given in an earlier chapter with the healing of a fever. It has been

Symbols and Powers

observed with other Masters also, but with Sai Baba, as might be expected, it took a spectacular and even bizarre form. He complained once of a fearful pain in the abdomen and bade the devotees wind a cloth round and pull it tight. 'Tighter! tighter! I can't bear it! The pain is frightful!' Then suddenly he relaxed. 'All right, the pain is gone now.' And it transpired that a lady devotee had been having a painful delivery and had called on Sai Baba for help.

One certain thing is that he had the most detailed knowledge of distant events and circumstances. Also it is certain that, whether he directed the actions of some other person or himself materialised in a distant body and played a part there, he could do so without going into a trance, which means without any interruption of his normal activities at Shirdi. He did not suffer from the illusion that he was the body and therefore there was no reason why he should be bound to it or should not be able to assume another body at will. This is a matter for scholars and theorists to argue about. His devotees do not need to ask such questions: they received and receive his favours in full faith.

CHAPTER FIVE

THE SYMBOLISM OF MONEY

A Holy man does not normally ask for money. There have been spiritual healers who have been given powers by their Guru with the express warning that if they accepted any rewards the powers would leave them. Many sadhus refuse even to touch money. Sri Ramakrishna had such a horror of it that he felt an actual burning in his hand if he touched it. Many people are suspicious of a Guru who accepts money or indeed any presents except simple things like fruit and flowers. In this, as in most things, Sai Baba was different. He not only accepted money but asked for it. Sometimes the demand for *dakshina* (alms) was the first thing he uttered to a visitor. Often, too, he specified the exact sum he required.

Some people were prejudiced against him because of this. It seemed so incongruous. What was the explanation? It was certainly not that he wanted the money, because he never kept it. He supported fakirs and other poor devotees, fed those who had no means to stay at Shirdi, squandered money on anything that came to hand, but never kept it. The word 'squandered' also must be qualified: it is true in the sense that he bought things that were not strictly necessary and that, if someone was attached to money, he would give it away right and left in front of his eyes, but it does not mean that he paid reckless prices. On the contrary, he would haggle over a piece of cloth in true market style though he might afterwards make a free donation to the vendor. He himself continued to beg his food. He never possessed luxury articles, founded an ashram, erected buildings or acquired property, and when he died he had just enough to pay for his funeral.

He regarded money, like everything else, symbolically, and for those who gave him it were laying up a better treasure for themselves. He did not ask all. He said once: 'I ask only those whom the Fakir points out, and in exchange I have to give them ten times as much.' They were his people and by accepting alms he was taking responsibility for them.

There were cases when he refused money, though offered, as when a man who was leading an immoral life came and offered him Rs. 500. He burst out: 'I want none of your money. You are keeping a woman in your house, aren't you? Give it to her.'

On the other hand, he might demand money just because it was wrongly come by. For instance, the lawyer, S. B. Dhumal, received Rs. 300 in fees for an appeal that he filed on behalf of some followers of Sai Baba. The appeal was granted immediately, through no effort on his part, by Sai Baba's influence. When he next went to Shirdi, Sai Baba repeatedly asked him for *dakshina* until he had taken the exact sum of Rs. 300 from him.

The same Dhumal (the devotee whose views are quoted at the end of Chapter Two) relates another story of *dakshina*. 'On one occasion, after taking all the money I had, Baba asked me for another Rs. 50. When I told him that I had no more money he told me to go and ask somebody for it. I did, but this person refused. I told Baba and he sent me next to Rao

Bahadur Sathe, who was overjoyed at the request. I did not know the significance of this at the time but found out much later that his claim for a pension was at that time being considered and that there was some doubt whether it would be based on the salary he drew in his last permanent appointment or would be Rs. 50 higher on the basis of a *pro tem* appointment he had held. If was finally granted at the higher rate, the order to this effect being passed on the very day that Sai Baba asked him through me for this fifty rupees. He immediately divined this and regarded the request as a demand for the first fruits of the new pension. That was why he was so pleased.'

Sai Baba not infrequently took all that a person had and then sent him away to borrow more. He certainly knew when he did this; it was not a question of guessing. Once, for instance, a visitor came with twenty rupees of which he gave eighteen to a friend to keep for him, so that if asked he could give two rupees and then truthfully say that he had no more. Sai Baba first asked him for two rupees and then for eighteen and, anticipating his reply, pointed to the friend and said, 'You can take it from him.'

The payment of first fruits was a frequent basis of his demands. This is a common practice, not only in India, a symbolical consecration of a man's new resources. Once two new Brahmin visitors arrived and Sai Baba told his devotee Deshpande to collect Rs. 15 from one of them. The other offered Rs. 35 unasked but he refused it. When Deshpande asked why, he explained: 'I do nothing. I receive nothing. God called for His own. This Rs. 15 was due, so it has been

The Symbolism of Money

collected, but the Rs. 35 was not ours, so it has been returned.' It turned out that the visitor who had paid the Rs. 15, who was then earning a good salary of Rs. 700 a month, had first started work on a salary of Rs. 15 and had vowed his first month's salary to a temple but had never made the payment, so it was now demanded of him.

Such unfulfilled vows as well as first fruits were a frequent reason for demands. For instance, a devotee who was on his way to Shirdi met another who gave him a coconut to present to Sai Baba and two annas to buy sugar for him. On taking leave he presented the coconut but forgot the two annas. Sai Baba said: 'Yes, you may go, but why keep back a poor Brahmin's two annas?'

The devotee at once remembered and gave him the two annas. Sai Baba then said, laughing: 'You may go now, but whatever you undertake to do, do it thoroughly; or don't undertake it at all.'

Again it might happen that a demand for money was simply to test a man's character. A sadhu was once asked for five rupees and restored angrily: 'You ask other people for *dakshina*, Baba, but why do you ask me? You know that I have no money.'

'All right,' Baba retorted coolly, 'then don't give it, but don't lose your temper'.

A rich but avaricious man once came to Sai Baba and demanded a vision of God. 'I have come all this long journey for it. They say that the Saint of Shirdi reveals God quickly.'

A spiritual experience much prized by some Hindus is a vision of God in whatever form they worship Him, as Rama or Krishna, the Divine Incarnations, or as Mother Kali or any other form. It is told in the Bhagavad Gita how Krishna thus gave Arjuna a vision of his awe-inspiring divine form but warned him afterwards that that was not the ultimate truth, that really he was beyond form. Such a vision can be a great encouragement to an aspirant, and a Guru can and often does bestow it. On the other hand, it can also be a limitation, since all form is ultimately illusory. It can turn a man from the quest of Formless Truth. Therefore, the Guru who teaches a direct and purely spiritual path usually deprecates such desires and refuses to gratify them. This was Sai Baba's attitude, and a number of devotees who asked for visions were disappointed. In fact, despite his spectacular and erratic behaviour, Sai Baba consistently discouraged sensationalism in his devotees. He wanted spiritual development, not visions or powers. Once a devotee came to him who had acquired certain magical powers from a former Guru and Sai Baba insisted on his renunciation of them. He himself never gave powers to his followers. Wisdom is required and complete freedom from egoism to use them worthily.

In the present case the visitor had driven from the railway station by *jetka* and was anxious to obtain his experience and return without having to pay the cabman for waiting at Shirdi. He had Rs. 250 in his pocket but hoped to keep it there safely. Sai Baba received him with mock enthusiasm. 'Oh yes, don't worry; I'll show you God quickly and clearly. This isn't a matter that can be delayed. People like you who seek

The Symbolism of Money

illumination are hard to find. Most people who come here want prosperity or health or freedom from some trouble or they want a good position or pleasure or some worldly object. Nobody wants God. How I long to see those who long to see God! One should realize Brahman before death or there will be an ever recurring cycle of births and deaths. A Guru can give realization and only a Guru can.'

Then he suddenly broke off and, calling to a boy, sent him with a message to a local shopkeeper that he urgently needed a loan of five rupees. The boy was to bring it back with him immediately. Until he returned, Baba seemed unwilling to occupy himself with the visitor or with any other matter. After a while the boy came back to say that the shopkeeper was not at home. Baba then sent him to another person and then another, each time without success. Meanwhile the visitor was getting more and restive, thinking of the cabman's fare. Of course, he could have cut short the delay by himself taking out the five rupees and giving it, but this he was not prepared to do.

'Will you help me to grasp Brahman?' he pleaded again.

And then Sai Baba explained the symbolism to him. 'But that is what I have been doing. Don't you understand? I want five. One must surrender five to attain Brahman. One must surrender the five senses and the five *pranas*, and for that one requires detachment. The road to *Brahman Jnana* (Divine Knowledge) is hard to tread. Not all can tread it. When it dawns there will be light. Only one who is unattached to things earthly and heavenly alike can attain Divine Knowledge.'

Not only was this a rebuke for his avarice (things earthly) but for his desire for a vision (things heavenly) also.

A somewhat similar instance is reported when Sai Baba again used the symbolism of money to expose the faulty basis of a petition to know God. This time he interrupted the talk to send to a local moneylender for a hundred rupees. The moneylender sent back his respectful greetings but not the money. Messages were sent to several others also but with no better result. Finally, Sai Baba turned, to a wealthy devotee for help and the latter, having no money with him at the moment, wrote out a promissory note and at once obtained the required amount from one who had refused Sai Baba.

Puzzled and resentful, the visitor later approached a regular devotee and expressed surprise that Sai Baba should have been so preoccupied with money as to forget his request. The devotee replied: 'He answered your request. You should have understood the symbolism. When a poor man asked for money it was not forthcoming but as soon as Nana Sahib asked for it he got it. Similarly, not every one can ask for Divine Knowledge—he must have accumulated the wealth of spiritual achievement first.'

To a large extent the devotees learned to understand the symbolism or grasped its meaning intuitively, but even they did not always agree about Sai Baba's demands for money. The following story shows how three different explanations could be given.

Sai Baba had asked a visitor for *dakshina* repeatedly until he left him penniless. He then asked him for more and sent

The Symbolism of Money

him to Deshpande to borrow it. Deshpande explained: 'It is not your rupees that Baba wants but your mind and heart, your time and the devotion of your soul.'

Sai Baba smiled approvingly when he heard the explanation but he sent him again, this time to Dixit. Dixit explained that the demand was merely an attack on his self-esteem so that he should not feel humiliated at being left penniless and forced to beg.

Sai Baba approved, this answer also but sent him a third time, this time to Nana Sahib Chandorkar. Nana Sahib was the most wordly wise of the three. He explained that it was his practice to bring only a hundred rupees to Shirdi and leave another hundred at the neighbouring town of Kopergaon so that he could send for it in case of need and thus avoid the inconvenience and humiliation of being left penniless. This doctrine of relying on one's own resources did not please Sai Baba and he immediately gave Nana a lesson. Sending for him, he demanded forty rupees. Hardly had Nana left when he sent after him for another forty. Nana immediately sent off to Kopergaon for his reserve fund, but before it could arrive Baba again asked him for *dakshina*, making him confess that he was penniless.

In many cases, however, the symbolism was clear. He repeatedly asked one devotee for two rupees, and when the latter finally asked him why, he said: 'It is not these two rupees of metal that I want but faith and patience.'

On another occasion he asked for four rupees but, on receiving it, said he had received only one.

'But I gave you four!' the devotee protested.

'I don't deny that; you gave four but I received only one.'

The devotee confessed that he did not understand but Sai Baba only replied that he would later. Some time afterwards the same man was travelling by train when a young fakir came into the compartment and asked for alms He gave him one pice (quarter anna) but the fakir asked for four. Then he gave a four anna piece but the fakir said he had received only one. Later he met an old sadhu who asked for alms and the same theme was repeated: he gave him one coin but the Sadhu asked for four. Finally he tumbled to the symbolism of it. Sai Baba was asking for the surrender of the four aspects of consciousness: *manas* (mentality), *buddhi* (intuitive intellect), *Chitta* (awarenesss) and *ahankara* (ego-sense), but was receiving only one, the soul or *jiva*.

On one occasion Sai Baba asked a lady for six rupees and she, having no money with her, turned to her husband and remarked how embarrassing it was to be asked for money and be unable to pay. 'Don't worry,' he replied; 'it is not money that Baba wants. It is the six vices that have to be surrendered to him.'

Smiling approval at the explanation, Sai Baba again asked her whether she would give him her six rupees and she replied that she had already done so. 'Then see that you do not go astray,' he cautioned her.

Symbolism such as this, payment of first fruits, fulfilment of a forgotten vow, these were the most frequent reasons for Sai Baba's demands for money. One thing was certain, that

The Symbolism of Money

it was not the money that he wanted. To that no one could have been more indifferent. Nevertheless, in the last years of his life an extraordinary flow of money did come in. It was said that his income equalled that of the Governor of a Province. Indeed, the authorities wanted to levy income tax on it, but as Sai Baba never had anything left by the end of the day it proved impossible. They did, however, levy income tax on several of his pensioners, poor followers to whom he gave a more or less regular allowance.

CHAPTER SIX

UPADESA

THE CENTRAL theme in the life of a Master is his *upadesa* (or *upadesh*, as it is commonly called), that is the spiritual guidance which he gives to his disciples. This is not theoretical or doctrinal instruction but a spiritual discipline normally consisting of rites and observances and the invisible influence that furthers the disciple's development. Although the central theme, it is not the most obvious or the easiest for the biographer to discover. In fact, it may be kept secret, since it is intended only for those to whom it is personally and directly transmitted, whereas any exposition of doctrine that the Master may make, being less potent and therefore less dangerous if misused, is open and for all. This encourages the mistaken attitude referred to in the first chapter of this book of representing a Spiritual Master as a mere philosopher. With Sai Baba, as already remarked, this is not possible, since he wrote no philosophy. Even verbally he rarely expounded doctrine. Very few of his devotees recall his doing so.

There are a number of different spiritual paths, and the question arises which Sai Baba enjoined. We may straight away discard yoga and tantra. This may seem strange, since it is these indirect paths which normally lead to the development of supernatural powers, However, it must be remembered, as remarked in a previous chapter, that although Sai Baba used his powers so lavishly, he did not bestow them on his devotees or encourage their development. Indeed, the lack of interest in developing powers among his devotees is one of the reassuring signs of his genuine spirituality. Wherever one finds disciples hankering after powers or equating their acquisition with spiritual progress it is advisable to be very wary of the Guru.

Sai Baba even deprecated *pranayama* or breath-control, which is much used on yogic and tantric paths, 'Whoever proceeds by means of *pranayama* will have to come to me ultimately for further progress.' This recalls the supreme Advaitin, Bhagavan Ramana Maharshi, who taught that breath-control is only a preliminary means of attaining thought-control for those who cannot do so directly; also his saying:, 'In the end all men must come to Arunachala', where Arunachala represents the direct path of *Jnana*.

It is also noticeable that Sai Baba did not wish his followers to renounce the world and go forth as *sanyasis* or mendicants. There were a few cases of his actually forbidding this but, even apart from that, the general interest he showed in the family life and problems of his devotees, their jobs, marriages and children, is clear evidence that he wished them to develop inwardly through the medium of family life.

There is also no record, however, of his prescribing the methods of *bhakti marga* or *jnana marga,* that is of devotion or Knowledge. In fact, he did not give initiation and *upadesa* in the usual manner at all. Some devotees have explicitly confirmed this. Prof. Narke says: 'Sai Baba never gave me any mantra, tantra or *upadesa* and so far as I know he gave them to nobody.' He also tells the following story on the authority of Deshpande.

A lady, by name Radnabai Deshmukhin, was in attendance on Sai Baba at Shirdi and wanted *upadesa*. When he did not give her any she started *satyagraha*, that is she stopped eating and determined not to take food until Sai Baba gave her *upadesa*. On the fourth day of her fast Deshpande, taking pity on her, went and told Sai Baba about it and besought him to give her some Name of God on which to call as *japa* (invocation) or *mantraupadesa*. Sai Baba then sent for her and told her that it was not his way to give *upadesa*, that he followed his Guru who was very powerful and whose methods were different and did not involve verbal *upadesa*.

Mrs. Manager reports the same. 'Sri Sai Baba's methods of giving spiritual help were not the usual ones. He gave no mantra (incantation) or *upadesa*. He never spoke of yoga, *pranayama* or *kundalini*. But when anything went wrong with anyone who was following any such *marga* (path) he would come to Sai Baba and would be helped.'

Nevertheless, he made it clear to his devotees that there was no need for them to go elsewhere in search of *upadesa*. Few even considered the question. His spiritual support was too potent and evident. H. V. Sathe has said: 'Baba never gave *upadesa* or initiation to anyone, so I did not ask him. On several occasions I was invited to obtain *upadesa* from someone else. On every such occasion I referred the question to Sai Baba and he gave a negative reply.' This is strongly reminiscent of Bhagavan Ramana Maharshi who also did not give initiation and *upadesa* as usually understood and yet, when asked by a devotee whether it was necessary to seek elsewhere, replied that it was not.

Upadesa

The extreme importance of this question becomes clear when one remembers that, in Hinduism and esoteric Islam, as in other religions, it is held that spiritual attainment during the life on earth is possible (except in the rarest of cases) only through initiation and *upadesa* by one who has himself attained. It can be regarded as the transmission of a current or as birth to a spiritual parent. To one who has grasped the possibility of spiritual attainment life holds no other goal. No human purpose can compare with that which transcends the human state. Therefore the vital importance of recognizing a true Guru and being accepted by him. Not every spiritual man even is a qualified Guru. Except in the case of a Maharshi or originator to a path, the authorisation must have been transmitted to him in an unbroken chain from Guru to Guru, like the ordination of an esoteric priesthood. One who is not a Guru may benefit mankind by his mere existence, by the radiation of an influence; there are other possibilities also; but he will certainly not take on himself the responsibility of guiding disciples or detaining them from others who can function as guides. If such a one as Sai Baba or the Maharshi took this responsibility it means then an invisible type of *upadesa* was in use whether the disciples were aware of it or not. And Sai Baba did assert in plain terms his responsibility for his devotees, his watch over them and the absolute reliance they could place in him. He said: 'I will never allow one of my people to escape from me'; and the Maharshi said: 'Just as the prey that has fallen into the jaws of a tiger will never be allowed to escape, so he who has won the Grace of the Guru will never to abandoned.' Sai Baba said: 'Only keep quiet and I will do the rest' and Maharshi said the very same words, only using the impersonal 'Bhagavan' instead of 'I'. Sai Baba said: 'Wherever you may be, think of me and I am with you.' Again, there was the same assurance though in slightly different words.

That Sai Baba did exert a tremendously powerful influence over his devotees there is no doubt at all. Many have testified to the awakening and fostering of spiritual life in them. Certainly he strove for them. He practised the laying on of hands. 'Baba had a way of touching the head of a devotee who went to him... His touch conveyed certain impulses, forces, ideas. Sometimes he pressed his hand heavily on the head as though crushing out some of the lower impulses of the devotee. Sometimes he tapped the head or made a pass over it with his hand. Each such action had its own effect, causing a remarkable change in the sensations or feelings of the devotee.'

Sai Baba was in fact training his devotees to seek God through devotion to the Guru. It will be remembered from the account given in the first chapter of this book that this was the method he himself had followed, and it was this that he enjoined on his followers. That this was his *upadesa* can be seen also from his exposition of a verse of the Bhagavad Gita quoted in Chapter One, where he said that complete surrender of body, mind, soul and possessions was the necessary means of attaining Realization. It is epitomised by Prof. Narke: 'Obeying, serving and loving God are the chief features of *bhakti marga*. The peculiar feature stressed by Sai Baba's example and words is the vast importance of developing this devotion on the basis of devotion to one's Guru. It is seeing God in, through and as the Guru, identifying the Guru with God'.

Upadesa

This is a legitimate and traditionally recognized method. Here again, it recalls the Maharshi, who said: 'God, Guru and Self are not really different; they are the same'. However, he added a safeguard by explaining that the outer Guru serves only to awaken the inner Guru in the heart of the devotee. And it will be seen that the 'Inner Guru' is the same as the Christian conception of the 'Christ in you'. Sai Baba explained less but there is a record of his also stressing the inner Guru when he said, in apparent contradiction of his own teaching: 'It is not necessary to have a Guru. Everything is within us. What you sow you reap. What you give you get.' The actual meaning is the relative unimportance of the outer Guru once the inner Guru can be recognized and heard. He continued still more explicitly: 'It is all within you. Try to listen inwardly and follow the direction you get.' It is important to note, however, that he did not say this to everyone; it is a very dangerous practice until the devotee is sufficiently purified and developed to follow the inner Guru, because all manner of selfish promptings can slip into the stream of consciousness and advertise themselves as inner spiritual direction. That is why normally, an outer Guru remains necessary.

Normally, Sai Baba's teaching was simply devotion to the Guru and complete surrender to him; a very potent method but one which can be safely used only by the perfect Guru from whom all trace of ego has been burnt out; otherwise a frightful danger. Sai Baba theorised little about it because in general he theorised little. The following story illustrates it well enough.

A devotee was staying at the house of Ayi, a woman devotee permanently resident at Shirdi to whom Sai Baba often sent visitors. He says: 'We agreed that *japa* (invocation) was the best course for us. The important question was what name we should use for it. She said that many used a name such as Vittal or Ram but so far as she was concerned Sai was her God and that name was enough for her. I said that what was good for her was good for me too and that I also would take the name of Sai. So we sat facing each other and repeating the name together for about an hour. Later in the day Sai Baba sent for me and asked me what I had been doing that morning.

"*Japa*," I replied.

"Of what name?" he asked

"Of my God."

"Who is your God ?" he asked next.

'I simply replied, "You know," and he smiled and said, "That's right," Thus *japa* of his name was expressly approved by him and perhaps silently instigated by him through the mediation of Ayi.'

It seems equally significant in this story that the invocation of his name was approved by Sai Baba and that it was approved secretly, not publicly. His position was already anomalous through the ritualistic worship performed by the Hindus and condemned by the Muslims, but a no less important distinction was between those Hindus who were following a spiritual path through devotion to God manifested as the Guru and those more numerous who simply accepted the spiritual and material benefits that accrued from the presence of a saint.

Upadesa

This type of *sadhana* or spiritual path though utter reliance on the Guru has been well summarised by Prof. Narke.

'According to the tradition of Sai Baba, the disciple or devotee who comes to the feet of a Guru in complete surrender has, no doubt, to be pure, chaste and upright, but he does not need to continue any active practice of *japa* or meditation. On the contrary, any such practice or any intellectual process which involves the postulate "I am doing this" is a handicap. All sense of *ahankara* or ego in the devotee has to be wiped out, swept out of the memory and mind, as it is an obstruction to the Guru's task. The Guru does not teach, he radiates influence. This influence is poured in and is absorbed with full benefit by the soul which has completely surrendered itself, blotting out the self, but it is obstructed by mental activity, by reliance on one's own exertions and by every kind of self-consciousness and self-assertion.

'This great truth must have been grasped by all observant visitors to Sai Baba. He himself sometimes said to devotees: "Stay with me and keep quiet. I will do the rest." – that is secretly and inwardly...

'So the duty of a devotee or aspirant is firstly to keep himself chaste, pure, simple and upright, so as to be fit to receive the Guru's Grace, and secondly to have full faith in the beloved Master to raise him to various higher and higher experiences till at last he is taken to the distant goal, whatever that may be. 'One step enough for me' is the right attitude for him now. He need not trouble to decide upon complicated metaphysical and philosophical problems about ultimate destiny. He is as yet ill prepared to solve them. The Guru will lift him up, endow him with higher powers, vaster knowledge and increasing realization of Truth. And the end is safe in the Guru's hands.

'All this was not uttered by Sai Baba at one breath either to me or within my hearing, but the various hints I got from his dealings with people and his occasional words about it add up to this. And common sense points the same way.'

This is an excellent synopsis of the *upadesa* of Sai Baba and it is perhaps natural that his devotee should give it a universal air as though it applied in all cases. It does not, of course. Meditation does not necessarily involve the postulate 'I am doing this'. In particular the enquiry 'Who am I ?' taught by the Maharshi does not; it enquires who is doing this. Also, no complicated metaphysical or philosophical problems are involved in envisaging the ultimate goal, which is simple Advaita, Oneness with the Absolute, and the Maharshi, for instance, expected his devotees to envisage this from the outset. Neither is it necessarily true that the Guru endows the devotee with ever higher powers, vaster knowledge and increasing realization of the Truth: the process may take place in darkness up to the final Self-realization.

Also, it needs to be said that to remain receptive to the Guru's influence in perfect purity and uprightness, to 'keep quiet' so that he can 'do the rest', is no easy task. In fact, it is the most difficult thing for the mind to do, and the purpose of meditations or invocations may be precisely to attain and maintain this purity and tranquillity of mind.

Those who are unused to such teaching may be alarmed at the emphasis laid on passivity, regarding it as dangerous or as leading to spiritual emasculation; but it is not. Passivity

Upadesa 87

to evil and to the ego is dangerous. Passivity to the senses and sense impulses leads to a gradual disintegration of character. Passivity to Truth and to a spiritual influence leads to integrity and power. That is why one sees that the saint, who is of all men the most submitted to the Divine will and the most lacking in ego, is at the same time the most dominant and outstanding in character, the most individual because he has sacrificed his individuality. Passivity towards God makes a man active or powerful towards the world. Passivity towards the ego makes a man active or rebellious towards God; that is why, in the early stages, submission is so difficult. Three great and widely known Masters in recent times have been Sri Ramakrishna Paramahamsa, Sai Baba and Bhagavan Ramana Maharshi. Sri Ramakrishna taught at Belur outside Calcutta, shortly before Sai Baba was established at Shirdi; and when Sai Baba died disciples were already being drawn to the Maharshi on Arunachala Hill in the South. There could be no better example of the utter difference of temperament and aptitude than these Masters all three of whom were powerful and dominating and all supremely passive to the Divine Will.

Several times already attention has been drawn to similarities between the paths laid down by Sai Baba and the Maharshi. There are similarities with Ramakrishna also and, considering the differences of temperament mentioned above, this can be interpreted only to mean that certain methods are recognized by the Masters as suitable to the times in which we live. It is of the utmost importance, therefore, to see what they are.

In the first place, all three upheld the equal validity of all religions. In previous ages, when each religion was more or less confined to its own parish, this was matter of little practical importance. The average Christian had heard nothing of Buddhism, nor the average Buddhist of Christianity. But with the rise of the modern one-world civilisation materialists and rationalists began to point to the differences between religions as an argument for regarding them all as erroneous and man-made. And since mankind in general came to know something of the various religions this was a dangerous argument. Superficial champions of one religion who denounced others were playing into the hands of the destroyers, whose very theme was that each religion claimed different and conflicting truth. It was for those of real insight to uphold that Truth is One and that only the modes of its expression vary. After attaining realization through Hinduism, Ramakrishna followed the path again, first through Islam and then through Christianity, and proclaimed that both led him back to the same goal. Sai Baba, as we have seen, had trod both the Islamic and the Hindu way and guided disciples on both, compelling each to recognize the validity of the other. Ramana Maharshi was above all religions, at the peak to which they ascend, the centre from which they radiate. Among his devotees were Christians, Muslims, Jews, Buddhists, Parsis as well as Hindus, and he never expected any to change from one religion to another.

Perhaps the most important consideration is that a path suited to modern times should be invisible, unencumbered by ritual, capable of being followed in the conditions of modern life, in the office or workshop well as the hermitage. There are many sincere aspirants who have to live a business or professional life with no facilities for ritualistic observances;

they have to follow their path inconspicuously among their colleagues, conforming to modern social conditions. This has been provided for. One is apt to think of the followers of Ramakrishna as ochre-robed Swamis, but it must be remembered that the Ramakrishna Mission, to which these Swamis belong, was founded after his death. During his lifetime he often refused permission for a devotee to renounce the world, as, for instance, in the case of Durgacharan Nag whose biography the Ramakrishna Math at Madras has published, considering him to be a saint. We have seen in the present book how Sai Baba encouraged family life. There were fakirs and sadhus among his followers but those who were householders when they first came to him remained such. The Maharshi also consistently refused requests of his devotees to be allowed to renounce the world and go forth as sadhus.

It is not only a question of remaining a householder but also of simplicity and in fact invisibility of the path followed. The method of Self-enquiry taught by the Maharshi requires no outer observances but can be followed inwardly. Sai Baba, as has been shown, prescribed no ritual or incantations. Sri Ramakrishna also taught no elaborate ritual. In all three cases, striving is largely through devotion to Guru. For most of their devotees this overshadows everything. 'Keep still and I will do the rest.' The tremendous power of the Guru is working; all that the disciple has to do is to refrain from obstructing it.

CHAPTER SEVEN

DEATH AND SURVIVAL

There was a rehearsal of Sai Baba's death as early as 1886. He said to Mahalsapathy, a devotee already referred to who resided permanently at Shirdi and slept beside him at the mosque: 'I am going to Allah. Take care of this body for three days. If I return I will look after it myself. If not bury it in that open land over there and put up two posts to mark the place.'

His breathing and circulation stopped. His heart stopped beating. The civil authorities held an inquest and pronounced him dead and ordered Mahalsapathy to bury or cremate the body, in accordance with the law that a body is not to be kept longer than twenty-four hours. Mahalsapathy, of course, refused. On the third day breathing began again and the abdomen was seen to move. Then Sai Baba opened his eyes and returned to life.

It was after this, in fact from about 1900, that his fame began to spread widely. From about 1910 till his death in 1918 there were unending streams of visitors from Bombay other towns. They forced pomp and ceremony on him that he did not want: processions with horses and elephants, a silver chariot, incense and singing. During the processions they loaded him with jewellery. They treated him like a Maharajah and like the idol of a God. He disliked all this but they would not be refused. Still he continued to go out and beg his food.

Death and Survival

His health gradually weakened. He suffered badly from asthma. The striving for his devotees was strenuous, because a Guru takes the burden on himself. Even physically it may be so with the performance of cures.

On Vijaya Dasami day in 1916 he had an attack of frenzy when he tore off his clothes and went about stark naked for two hours, crying out that it was his day of 'crossing the frontiers'. It was on the same day two years later, 15 October by the Western calendar, that he breathed his last.

Before going he sent some devotees back to Bombay, who had intended to stay, and detained others who were due to leave. He bade farewell to one who used to pay him fortnightly visits and told him not to continue coming. None seem to have grasped the point of these dispositions. He sent word to another Muslim saint: 'The light that Allah lit he is taking away', and the saint received the message with tears. He gave two hundred rupees for feeding fakirs and they sat chanting prayers and reading the Quran. It was the time of the Hindu feast of Dasara and the Rama Vijaya was read before him.

He had been sick for a few days, but those around him did not realize that it was the final sickness. In the morning he was ill. About midday he sat up and gave first five rupees and then four to the Brahmin who used to receive daily four rupees for preparing his food (for the food he begged was often uncooked and was cooked later at the mosque). He sent those who were with him out to take their lunch. Two Brahmins alone remained with him. One of them relates: 'Baba gave me his last instructions on the day he breathed his last. After sending Dixit away he gave me some instruction and told me to keep quiet about it, saying that I would die if I revealed it to anyone. Then he said: "I am going. Carry me to the *wada*. Only Brahmins will be near me." With these words he breathed his last. After these words were spoken Nana Nimonkar poured water into his mouth but it came out. I held my hand under his chin to catch the water. Baba expired leaning against me.'

Sai Baba was here using the word 'Brahmin' in its true meaning of 'spiritually inclined person', as he did, for instance, when he said, 'This is a Brahmin mosque'. By *wada* he referred to the building where he was to be buried, a large stone house built by Bapu Saheb Buty. Some years previously Sai Baba had appeared in a dream both to him and Deshpande the same night, desiring him to build it. When Buty asked his permission to do so he not only consented but said, 'When the temple is built we will live in it'. Once Sai Baba was no longer physically alive at Shirdi, Buty had no wish to occupy the newly completed building, so it was used, as its destiny had been, to house the shrine.

Despite Sai Baba's expressed wish, there was disagreement about his burial, the Muslim followers holding that he was one of them and should be buried by them in a building to be erected for the purpose. The civic authorities therefore circulated two petitions for signature and as more than double the number petitioned for burial in the *wada* this was done. It was agreed by both parties that both the *wada* and the mosque should be kept open for pilgrims of all religions.

The fire which Sai Baba always maintained is still kept burning at the mosque, but railings have now been put round

Death and Survival

it. The sacred ash is given out as before to devotees who desire it. Railings have also been put up at the entrance at the east end of the mosque. Sai Baba was fond of smoking tobacco from clay pipes which quickly broke or got foul and hundreds of which littered the mosque and its courtyard when he passed away. Many were taken away as relics and then the remainder were gathered up and cemented into a block which is kept in the mosque together with the water pot and coconut shell jug he used to use.

The *chavadi* or rest-house where, for a large part of his life, Sai Baba used to sleep every alternate night was a dismal mud structure like the original mosque, but a large part of it collapsed in 1916 and it was rebuilt in brick. A large portrait of Sai Baba is kept here.

It may be asked why Sai Baba's Hindu followers should have buried and not cremated the body. Actually, it is a tradition that the body of a Realized man should be buried. He has passed through the fire already; there is no need to do so symbolically after death.

There was something delusive about his death and burial because all knew that Sai Baba had not died. He was arranging his survival at the same time as his burial. Some two weeks beforehand, when they had no suspicion that death was approaching, he ordered R. B. Purandhare and H. S. Dixit to leave for Bombay, telling them: 'I will go on ahead and you can follow me. My tomb will speak. My clay will give you replies.' This should have been warning enough, but one must remember that Sai Baba's devotees were accustomed to hearing strange sayings from him.

A lady once told Sai Baba that she depended on him utterly for refuge and guidance and would be hopelessly adrift without him and asked him what she was to do when he passed away. He replied categorically: 'Wherever and whenever you think of me I shall be with you'.

Once again a parallel arises with Bhagwan Ramana Maharshi. When his death was approaching some devotees appealed to him in the same way and he replied tersely: 'You attach too much importance to the body.' The implication was obviously the same.

There was no change in Sai Baba's guidance of devotees, his answering of prayers and his protection in time of trouble. Indeed, so continuous is his influence that in hearing or reading accounts by his devotees of their experiences one does not find any dividing line at 1918, the same kind of episodes occurring before and after. And, of course, with most of the devotees one meets today all cases of intervention come from after that date. He appears to them in dreams and visions as before. They turn to him and receive his answer and protection. When decision is difficult they write out various solutions on slips of paper and, with a prayer for guidance, place them beneath his picture and accept the one they draw as his instruction. Invisibly he guides and influences them. He has said that no devotee of his shall lack for food or shelter and they have found it so. People turn to him in distress and find relief. And deeper down, beneath this gracious help in the storms of life, is the spiritual current maturing them to deeper and less tangible rewards.

A devotee has recorded how he visited another saint, Narayan Maharaj, in 1927, looking upon him as Sai Baba in a different form, still attached to Sai Baba but craving the consolation of a human presence to see and a human voice to answer him. He said nothing of all this but the saint told him: 'Yours is a supreme Guru. He is of a higher rank than me. Why have you come here? Your choice of a Guru is excellent. Go to him and you will achieve your purpose.'

Another tells how his child was sick with pneumonia in 1934 and had in addition an open abscess on the chest 'The doctor was afraid to operate on the abscess on account of his weakness. It was a wide, open wound. The doctor would not help me, so I relied on my own doctor, Sai Baba, and put a little of his *udhi* (sacred ash) into the wound. The Deputy Collector, V. R. M. Jadhav, asked me whether I was confident of a cure and within what time the gaping wound would be healed. I answered: "Within twenty-four hours." That night Sai Baba appeared to me in a dream and rebuked me, saying: "You should have said immediately." I apologized in my dream and when I woke up next morning the wound was healed. Jadhav was so surprised that he asked for some of Sai Baba's *udhi* for his own four-year-old son who was down with pneumonia. It was already the sixth day of his fever when I gave him the *udhi*, and the fever stopped next day although the doctor had told him it would take another three days.'

The same child who was cured of the abscess had already been saved by Sai Baba when he was two. He fell downstairs. There was a heap of debris at the bottom of the stairs and his father ran up to him in alarm. To his surprise he found the child quite unhurt. 'It's all right', the little one said, 'Baba held me up.'

These are old tales. Those one hears today are mostly from devotees who were born since 1918, but they are no less vivid and the help given is no less potent. None could be more categorical about this than Sai Baba.

'I shall remain active and vigorous even after leaving this earthly body.'

'My shrine will bless my devotees and fulfil their needs.'

'My relics will speak from the tomb.'

'I am ever living to help those who come to me and surrender and seek refuge in me'.

'If you cast your burden on me I will bear it.'

'If you seek my help and guidance I will immediately give you it.'

He said: 'There shall be no want in the house of my devotee.' It is because his succour has been found so prompt and potent that he has such vast numbers of devotees, now as in his lifetime, but it is good to remember also that other saying of his: 'I give people what they want in the hope that they will begin to want what I want to give them.'

CONTINUED PRESENCE

During our four year stay in Calcutta around 1960 the neighbouring flat was occupied by an old lady, Miss Dutton who was very pious. When we came to know her better she told me that she used to be a nun having spent the best part of her life in a convent. Being rather impulsive, a common thing with redheads, she found discipline increasingly irksome and this led to conflicts and unpleasantness. In short she did not get on at all with the other nuns. Towards the end she felt that she could not stand it any longer. With the co-operation of the nuns in charge she applied to the Pope for absolution from her vows which was granted without much delay. While her application was pending she was too preoccupied with her conflicts to give much thought to her future. When she was about to leave the convent it dawned on her how hopeless her future now was. She was well over middle age, without a profession with scarcely any relatives, the nearest being a nephew in faraway Calcutta. One day while sitting in her cell immersed in the deepest gloom, suddenly a tall fakir appeared before her. How he got in she could not tell as it would have been next to impossible for a Muslim fakir to gain entrance into a cell of a nun. He looked at her with compassion and told her: "Do not worry so much, everything will be all right when you go to Calcutta." Then he asked her for dakshina (a gift of money to holy men). She told him that she had no money. "Oh yes, you have 35 Rupees in a box in the cupboard there" he replied. "And do you know", she told me "I had completely forgotten about it". She went to the cupboard to get it and there it was but when she turned round with her gift, the fakir was not there. He just disappeared in the same way as he came in. She felt at peace.

In Calcutta her nephew received her very kindly and was looking after her with love and care which he extended even to her animal pets. He may still be doing so now. Miss Dutton was all praise for him and so grateful that she used to get up every day before dawn to go to Church to attend Mass or give thanks. This discipline she seemed to enjoy.

"I will show you a picture of your fakir". I told her convinced that it could have been none other than the incredible Sai Baba. Luckily, I fetched a picture of Sai Baba from our flat and showed it to the old lady who the moment she saw it exclaimed with surprise: "This is my fakir. He had even the same white kerchief on his head." She had never heard of Sai Baba before.